Burt Rutan

Aeronautical and Space Legend

Burt Rutan

Aeronautical
and Space Legend

By Daniel Alef

Meta4 Press, an imprint of Titans
of Fortune Publishing

ISBN-13: 978-1-60804-3330
ISBN-10: 1-60804-3339

Published by Meta4 Press, imprint of Titans of Fortune Publishing.
25 Hudson Street #210
Jersey City, NJ 07302
www.titansoffortune.com

Book Design: Neil Kottler
Cover Design: Ana Grigoriou

Library of Congress Control Number: 2016918968
Titans of Fortune Publishing, Goleta, CA

1. Aviation   2. Aviation History   3. Aviation Pioneers
4. Space   5. Space Pioneers   6. Entrepreneurs

Cover Image of White Knight One. Photo Courtesy of Mojave
Aerospace Ventures

PRAISE FOR DANIEL ALEF'S TITANS OF FORTUNE BIOGRAPHICAL PROFILES

"I've read these wonderful profiles with such pleasure...

—Barnaby Conrad, International best-selling author and founder of the Santa Barbara Writers Conference

"Your column on Otis Chandler was the best encapsulation of Otis I have ever seen."

—Marylin Chandler De Young, wife of Otis Chandler.

"I am a great fan of Titans of Fortune... Dan Alef has found a savvy combination of facts and feelings in selected bios

—Fred Klein, Former executive editor at Bantam Books.

"As a fellow lawyer and writer, I was impressed with your easy style and eye for detail, and fluid prose--two hallmarks of a good storyteller.

—Pierce O'Donnell, Author of *Fatal Subtraction* and *In Time of War*.

"A friend of mine, who lives in Santa Barbara, sent me the copy of Capt. Matson, that was printed in your paper. It was beautifully written and I will put it in my keepsakes. I am a granddaughter of the Capt.; my father was Walter Matson...

—Carol Park

"For a long time, I have enjoyed your essays. They are concise, well-written and informative. I think we do not tell writers often enough how much we appreciate their work, so I thought I would drop you a line.

—Mashey Bernstein, Lecturer, Writing Program at University of California at Santa Barbara

"It was fun to see you, especially as your mind was still churning Getty's life story, and then . . . bam, it was there. You have a great reportial touch.

—Doran William Cannon, Award-winning Hollywood screenwriter, author and founder of The Writers Academy

Kit process - P31

Burt Rutan

Aircraft Designer

TABLE OF CONTENTS

b. ~1943
d.

— INDEX ?

Author's Acknowledgment

I would like to thank Burt and Tonya Rutan for their generosity and hospitality in helping me prepare Burt's life story. Opening oneself to close scrutiny is never an easy task and brutally exhausting, but throughout our talks Burt showed patience and shared many wonderful stories, all manifestations of his character. He also reviewed several manuscripts to insure I got it right; that his story is factual and accurate. Burt is an American national treasure and I hope this biographical profile does him justice. Ultimately he will write his autobiography and then we will know the whole story.

Daniel Alef,
August 26, 2016

Oh! I have slipped the surly bonds of Earth
And danced the skies on laughter-silvered wings;
Sunward I've climbed, and joined the tumbling mirth
Of sun-split clouds, — and done a hundred things
You have not dreamed of — wheeled and soared and swung
High in the sunlit silence. Hov'ring there,
I've chased the shouting wind along, and flung
My eager craft through footless halls of air. . . .

Up, up the long, delirious burning blue
I've topped the wind-swept heights with easy grace
Where never lark, or ever eagle flew —
And, while with silent, lifting mind I've trod
The high untrespassed sanctity of space,
Put out my hand, and touched the face of God.

— John Gillespie Magee, Jr.

FOREWORD

The rise of the United States to the status of world superpower is coincident with and, at least in this author's opinion, due in large measure to the invention, development, and promotion of aviation and spaceflight by our nation in the 20th Century. The ability to project power, conduct commerce, and spread influence by these new means proved telling in both World War II and the Cold War, and indeed has reshaped human society in ways unimaginable to our great-grandparents. That the United States ultimately mastered the arts and sciences of flight in all its forms, if not always first, then clearly better than our competitors, is due to the efforts of a long line of creative engineers, courageous pilots, insightful military strategists, dedicated statesmen and, above all else, bold and visionary entrepreneurs who saw success where others could only see stumbling blocks.

Burt Rutan is, all by himself, many of these things. Any listing of some of the great names in aviation and space – the Wright brothers, Charles Lindberg, Jimmy Doolittle, Donald Douglas, Glenn Martin, Allan and Malcolm Loughead, Bill Boeing, Jack Northrop, Sandy McDonnell, Wernher von Braun, Max Faget, Chris Kraft, Alan Shepard, John Glenn, Neil Armstrong – that doesn't include "Burt Rutan" is automatically incomplete. If you're an aerospace "insider", you know that, of course. But more interestingly, while some of the people mentioned above are very well known to the general public, many others of equal professional stature are not well known outside of aviation and space. Burt Rutan is. He is one of those who is universally acknowledged by both casual observers and aerospace aficionados to be a true aviation and space pioneer. But even so, no one else is quite like Burt Rutan. To be the driving intellectual and organizational force behind the first non-stop, around-the-world flight with the *Voyager* aircraft, and then to do the same for the first privately-accomplished suborbital space flights in *Space Ship One* – no one else spans such a range.

The great engineers, the great designers, all have a "signature", a look or feel or characteristic of their work which is uniquely their own and is instantly recognizable as such, often even by laymen. The tube-and-wing airplane design pioneered by Donald Douglas with the DC-3 remains with us today, a unique legacy of the man who conceived the first practical air transport. The Mercury, Gemini, and Apollo spacecraft have "Max Faget" written all over them; the designs of his Cold War competitor Sergei Korolev are just as certainly *his* designs, each man solving the same problems of early spaceflight but with very different styles. And, just as certainly, the Starship, Voyager, White Knight, and Space Ship One could only have been created by Burt Rutan. If another engineer were to author a similar concept for a new air- or space vehicle, it would still – and forever – be known as "a Burt Rutan design".

The traits that make Burt a true American "original" in the field of aerospace vehicle design carry over into his larger world. He simply looks at things differently, and is unconvinced by any argument whose central theme relies upon conventional thinking. Thus, the received wisdom of the supposed "scientific consensus" on anthropomorphic global warming is anathema to Burt. He takes a different view of the phenomenon, can back his views with data rather than hyperbolae, and doesn't care whether he is disliked, or by whom, for his stance.

But if Burt is an original and sometimes even iconoclastic thinker, he is also a quiet, sometimes shy, man who deals with the fact of his singular accomplishments far more modestly than many who have offered far less. He carries himself with a genuine but quiet confidence, is rarely the first to speak out, and doesn't need to have everyone, or even anyone, in the room know that he is "Burt Rutan". The author of the work you are about to read will try to tell you who he is, how he came to be that way, and what he has accomplished with his amazing life. I hope you will enjoy it. But for me, the best thing I can say to you about Burt Rutan is that he is my friend.

Michael D. Griffin, Ph.D
September 13, 2011

Michael D. Griffin, an award-winning physicist and engineer, served as Administrator of NASA from 2005 to 2009. Before that he was head of the Space Department at the Johns Hopkins University Applied Physics Laboratory. Named by *Time* magazine as one of the 100 most influential people in 2008, Dr. Griffin was appointed eminent scholar and professor of mechanical and aerospace engineering at the University of Alabama in Huntsville. He is the author of numerous articles and the textbook "Space Vehicle Design." Dr. Griffin is also one of the initial directors of Stratolaunch Systems, Paul Allen's newest company devoted to developing the next generation of space travel.

Figure 1 Burt Rutan. Courtesy of Burt Rutan.

INTRODUCTION

Great American titans, good and bad, earned unusual sobriquets and interesting nicknames. Cornelius Vanderbilt was known as the "Colossus of Roads" for his massive railroad holdings; Hetty Green, the richest woman in American history who donned black dresses, was known as "the Witch of Wall Street"; Eddie Rickenbacker became the "Ace of Aces"; and Benjamin Franklin "the new Prometheus." However, few have ever been accorded as many names as Burt Rutan. *The Los Angeles Times* called him an "Aerospace Legend," the *Wall Street Journal* dubbed him "Space Pioneer." He was called the "Final Frontiersman" by *Popular Mechanics* and the "Magician of Mojave" by *Air and Space Magazine*. Paul Allen described him as "larger than life" and Sir Richard Branson sees him as "one of the world's true geniuses...an Einstein of aerodynamics."

Does Burt Rutan merit such accolades? Part of the answer could be his appearance on the cover of *Time*—twice—*Life, Wired, Inc., Aviation Week*, and other magazines. But a bigger part of the answer is at the Smithsonian's Air and Space Museum where four Rutan-designed airplanes and one spacecraft are on exhibit. SpaceShipOne, an air-launched suborbital manned spacecraft that was the first manned private spaceflight in history and won the Ansari X Prize, hangs between The *Spirit of St. Louis* and the Bell X-1 in the Milestones of Flight Gallery. A few hundred feet away is another record-shattering, Rutan-designed craft—Voyager—the first plane to circumnavigate the globe without stopping or refueling. More of his planes can be found in other air museums across the nation.

Among more than seventy medals and awards he has received so far, including the Presidential Citizen's Medal, are two Collier trophies and two Lindbergh medals; he's the only man in aviation history to be so honored by multiples of both prestigious awards. And his popularity in aviation circles is unprecedented. In 1998, owners of more than 120 Rutan-designed airplanes flew into Mojave Airport, in California's arid desert, to celebrate his fifty-fifth birthday. When he appears at the annual Experimental Aircraft Association (EAA) air show in Oshkosh, Wisconsin, the largest airshow—and convention—in the world, attended each year by half a million people, his fans swarm around him as if he were a rock star or famous movie actor.

Figure 2 Burt Rutan (with sideburns) mobbed by his fans at the 1978 EAA air show in Oshkosh, WI, almost concealing two of his aircraft. Courtesy of Burt Rutan.

His name may not yet be as well known to the general public as the Wright brothers or Charles Lindbergh, but one day it will be, perhaps in the next year or two, when Sir Richard Branson's Virgin Galactic begins taking paying passengers into suborbital space flights on the Rutan-inspired VSS *Enterprise*.

A tall, angular man with piercing pale-blue eyes, graying hair, still sporting his legendary mutton chop sideburns that trace back to Elvis Presley days, Burt Rutan has a confident mien that speaks volumes about his achievements. More so, he retains a warmth and charm that lead all who meet him to see a very humane and easy-going man who is as comfortable with Paul Allen and Sir Richard Branson as with the men in the shop. He cares as much about people as he does about his innovative and cutting-edge work. Having developed forty-five unique airplanes in forty-three years, many serving as proof-of-concepts, he established an unprecedented record: not a single crash or fatality in all the test flights. What makes this even more remarkable is that in many cases Burt had built only one prototype, while in the aviation business, most companies build two or three prototypes, sometimes more, in anticipation of testing failures.

But if anyone tries to give Burt credit for being the designer of all the craft he has been associated with, they are going to get an earful from a man who wants to give credit where credit is due. He designed many of the planes, not all of them, though he was intimately involved in their development. "I don't want to wait until I die for these guys to get credit," he told me. It's pretty obvious that placing Burt's name on any airplane design gets attention and makes a project more marketable. But when I mentioned that he designed Virgin Galactic's SpaceShipTwo he forcefully reminded me that Jim Tighe should get credit for its design. This is not false humility; it accurately portrays a man who achieved extraordinary success and can assess his achievements dispassionately. That is not to say he doesn't have an ego; he does. He just doesn't paint himself to be any larger than he really is.

CHILDHOOD AND EARLY YEARS

Elbert Leander Rutan was born June 16, 1943, on a farm outside Estacada, southeast of Portland, Oregon, on the edge of the Mt. Hood National Forest. His father, George Albert Rutan, known affectionately in family circles as "Pop," farmed a small tract of land owned by his maternal grandfather, and made improvements to the rustic nineteenth century two-story home with no plumbing where the family, including Burt's mother Irene, older brother Richard and sister Nellie lived. Burt's earliest memories are riding on a tractor on the farm or hearing dynamite explosions set off by his grandfather to clear the land.

When World War II began, Pop took jobs in Portland working in Henry Kaiser's shipyards building Liberty ships, and later with a sawmill and the Forest Service. The rough physical labor took its toll on Pop's back, and he was thinking of starting a new occupation when he received his draft notice. Despite having three young children, Pop joined the Navy and was assigned to the Hospital Corps at Camp Farragut in the Coeur d'Alene Mountains of Idaho. Irene temporarily rented a house in Coeur d'Alene and moved there with the children.

Pop's back problems, attributed to chronic arthritis, made him a full-time ward of the hospital until he was discharged just before Christmas 1944. Less than a year later, the family moved to Arlington, California, where Pop took some courses at Riverside Junior College before entering the School of Dentistry at the University of Southern California in Los Angeles. Burt found himself living with his family in a small mobile trailer before Pop gained access

Figure 3   Rutan Family in 1944. (left to right) Nellie, George, Richard, Burt and Irene. Courtesy of Burt Rutan.

to a primitive one-room university housing unit. Pop subsequently managed to get the family into the Estrada Gardens, a two-bedroom apartment in East Los Angeles that seemed luxurious compared to their previous accommodations.

After Pop's graduation, Burt's family moved to Orosi, in California's San Joaquin Valley, the state's fertile agricultural region, not far from where Pop had attended grammar school. The southern Sierra Nevada Mountains to the east tower over the flat verdant farmlands surrounding the small town where fields of row crops, cotton, and fruit orchards abound. Pop opened a dental office at nearby Dinuba with a $5,000 loan from Bank of America. As the dental practice thrived, Pop moved the family to Dinuba, a small town he felt was as ideal for raising a family. Looking for things to do in his spare time, Pop started taking flying lessons just before Burt's tenth birthday. By year's end, Pop had purchased a Model A Beech Bonanza with two friends.

Figure 4   Pop's Model A Beech Bonanza. Courtesy of Burt Rutan.

Burt didn't have to venture far to become interested in aviation; he was surrounded by it. In addition to Pop's Bonanza, his older brother, Dick, with whom Burt shared a room behind the garage, was immersed in aviation. When Burt was at the impressionable age of eleven, Dick turned sixteen and got his private pilot's license—the driver's license, almost an afterthought, came later that afternoon. "Flying was everything to Dick," Burt says.

There were other inspirations, like the time a formation of giant B-36 "Peacemaker" super bombers flew above his home, their engines—either the original six-engine craft or the ten-engine—four turbojets and six piston-driven ones—roaring like thunder. In either case it was an awesome sight to an impressionable boy. And in 1955 Walt Disney first aired Disneyland. Burt's parents were Seventh Day Adventists and not allowed to have TV sets, but Pop's friend in Orosi had one, and every Wednesday Burt would go there to watch TV. At 7:30 the TV would be turned to Disneyland on ABC, Channel 7. Beginning March 9, a new Disney series aired called *Man in Space*. One episode featured America's premier rocket scientist, Werner Von Braun, who discussed future missions to Mars. This really fired

Burt's imagination with flight, rockets, and space travel, and he expected to see man land on Mars in his lifetime, something he now finds dubious and improbable. Werner von Braun, one of the greatest rocket engineers in the history of flight, would serve as a role model for Burt as a scientist who demonstrated what could be achieved with analytics, brains, guts, creativity and vision.

Figure 5 (left to right) Dr. Heinz Haber, Werner von Braun, Willey Ley discuss Disney's Man in Space TV program. NASA.

The mid and late 1950s were the foundational years in Burt's interest in aviation. He began building and designing model planes. He first attended model plane shows when his father was getting his dental degree at USC. When some models crashed, Burt would ask the owners if he could take some of the broken parts, and later fashioned these pieces of balsa wood and other components into his own designed model planes. Even in the Pathfinders, the Adventist version of the Boy Scouts, he won a blue ribbon for building a model airliner out of balsa and silk span. It was big, but could not fly. It was a rather unique airliner because it had jet engines hanging off pylons on the wings, something that would be seen years later when Boeing introduced the 707. The only commercial airliner at the time was the Comet where the engines were in the wings, adjacent to the fuselage. "I wasn't interested in models for display; I was interested in models for flying," he said, "what makes planes fly well." He challenged himself by trying to set records and entering competitions.

Figure 6 Burt With Model of Pop's Bonanza and Trophy. Courtesy of Burt Rutan.

Model airplane competitions involve several categories, including scaled, control line, and free flight. Scaled models are judged by how closely they replicate the real airplanes. In control-line scaled competitions, the model is flown in a circle and controlled by a pilot in the center holding a handle with two thin steel wires leading to the model's wing tips. Points are also awarded for speed and slow flight. Burt excelled in all facets of model competition. Not only were his airplanes perfectly scaled models of the real planes, including Pop's Bonanza, he was an innovator who stunned the judges with his novel designs.

In a control-line Navy carrier competition, models took off and landed on a wooden replica of an aircraft carrier, "Burt built a plane that looked like a contemporary Navy fighter," Dick told Edwards Park of the *Smithsonian*. "Then he worked out how to do a power stall with it. The thing would almost hover over the deck, tail down, engine full on, until he dropped it at exactly the right spot and engaged the arresting gear. He always won." And in another scoring format, contestants were awarded a point for every second it took to fly seven laps—the slower the better—Burt would have his fighter hover in one place, the seconds ticking away, the points accumulating in his favor, leaving the judges puzzled and uncertain how to score him.

Burt used his $5 allowance judiciously, building a variety of models. Between 1956 and 1959 he entered the Western Associated Modelers competitions in San Francisco and surrounding areas. Getting up at 3:00 a.m. to get to the venue on time, he was driven there by the owner of Dinuba's hobby shop.

In 1959 and 1960 he entered national competitions, the first in Los Alamitos, California, and the second in Dallas, Texas. Burt was seventeen when he went to Dallas and entered nine different events. Coming from a little town, Burt was awed by the huge hangars at the venue, and the number of planes and competitors. He had two Nordic towline gliders and a Fairchild F-27 among other craft. The Fairchild won first place in the scaled control line competition. However, the Nordic gliders were emblematic of something much more enduring and apocryphal. Burt employed a system called dethermalizing that turned the tail up. Years later, after SpaceShipOne had flown successfully, someone told Burt the special feathered reentry system that made SpaceShipOne possible resembled the dethermalizing Burt employed with his 1960 Nordic gliders. Burt acknowledged that perhaps the inspiration for the feathered reentry came from something that had remained deeply ingrained in his subconscious mind for a number of decades.

Figure 7 "Flight of the Phoenix" with new plane fashioned by a model engineer from parts salvaged in crash.

This involvement with model planes morphed years later into an unprecedented career where he designed or developed forty-five unique aircraft (those that we know of since there may have been others that were shrouded in secrecy and not made public). It brings to mind "Flight of the Phoenix," the Robert Aldrich-directed movie starring James Stewart where a German model plane designer Heinrich Dorfmann conceives a design to fashion a new plane out of the wreckage of a crashed one. The unusual-looking craft Dorfmann designs rescues the passengers from certain death in the scorching Sahara. If that scenario seemed improbable or incredible at the time, imagine having seventeen-year-old Burt play that role. You could take the result to the bank.

Although the seeds of interest in aviation were firmly planted by 1957 between Pop's Bonanza, Dick's all-consuming interest in flying, and Burt's growing fleet of model planes, other events seem to have foreshadowed his future. Burt attended Dinuba Junior

Academy, an Adventist middle school. Seventh Day Adventists were not allowed to watch movies, but inexplicably the school showed one movie—the first motion picture Burt had ever seen—*The Spirit of St. Louis*, starring James Stewart. Released in 1957, the movie tells the story of Charles Lindbergh's remarkable feat: risking it all in tackling a solo crossing of the Atlantic. Burt was moved by the movie, but the subliminal message was lasting: Lindbergh's determination to seek new horizons and achieve the impossible. To top it off, Lindbergh was Dick Rutan's hero and years later Dick would emulate Lindbergh by setting records and being the first person to fly around the globe without stopping or refueling in the Voyager.

Burt also wanted to learn to fly and began taking lessons at Alta Airport, a 3,300-foot oiled hard-scrabble runway nestled between farms and orchards. Burt paid $4.50 for a fueled Aeronca Champ and the instructor, John Banks, the country western D.J. on local radio—who would sing songs like "El Paso" while Burt was flying. The typical lesson was only seven or eight minutes long—all Burt could afford—and consisted of flying one or two patterns. Pop provided Burt with an allowance and Burt had to be prudent about how he applied it to the lessons. Burt soloed after five hours and forty-five minutes of lessons, but would not get his private pilot's license until after graduating from college.

Burt attended Fresno Union Academy, an Adventist school for eighth and ninth grades before transferring to his first public school, Dinuba High School. In some ways he was the normal high school teen: he ran cross-country one semester, listened to Elvis Presley, and didn't devote himself to his studies. He had a crush on a girl, Darla Banks—his flying instructor's daughter who later won the first Miss Teen USA contest. And like most teenagers, he pressed the limits of the rules set by his parents, sneaking out occasionally to see a movie, the first time with his cousin Jerry Hoy to watch *High Noon*, though to avoid being caught or recognized they sat in the balcony, and at another time with a friend to see *On The Beach*. In other ways Burt was different from the kids at school. He did not have a car; he was not really interested in cars; he did not like rock music, and his socializing revolved around model planes. He joined the Academy of Model Aeronautics, a model-airplane club which held its competitions on Saturday, a problem Burt had to overcome since Saturdays were the Adventist day of rest and the competitions were against his religion.

Like titans before him who could recall a teacher who had considerable influence in their formative years, Burt remembers Martin Goehring's physics class taken in his senior year. "It opened my eyes . . . to a world of fascinating stuff. . . . he made a big impression on me, convincing me to be an engineer, not a dentist like Pop." What he learned in that class not only influenced his interest in engineering, it was the spark that ignited part of his current views on CO2 and its impact on global warming. He also recalls his typing class where he was the only boy taking a class designed to provide girls with the tools they would need to become secretaries. It still accounts for the speed with which his fingers blaze across the keyboard today, an ability that he has put to good use since high school. Perhaps his public speaking class ended up the most indispensible since Burt is now a keynote speaker at many major events and for large corporations, universities, and other organizations.

COLLEGE YEARS

As the summer of 1961 approached, Burt knew he did not have enough credits to graduate, so he enrolled in summer classes at Fresno State, intent on graduating and getting into college. California Institute of Technology would have been his top choice, but he did not have the grades, so he applied to one school, California Polytechnic University at San Luis Obispo, known as CalPoly. The university had a highly regarded aerodynamics department in the school of engineering and Burt planned to pursue a degree in aeronautical engineering. Given his lackluster high school record he barely squeaked into the program.

The first year at CalPoly was a difficult time for Burt. He married his high school girlfriend Judy Prather and could no longer live in a dormitory. Burt and Judy moved into a trailer park and subsequently into "Vetville," an old box apartment in campus married housing where rent was $35 a month. Probably unhappy with such an early marriage, Pop did not provide much financial support for the newly-weds, something Pop would rue years later. "Boy, I was on my own," Burt acknowledged. He was carrying a huge yoke of responsibility on his shoulders: taking a rigorous academic work load, supporting himself and his wife, paying for school, and holding part-time jobs. Any thought of taking more flying lessons was out of the question.

His first job was in a bakery, where he would go to work well before dawn, wash dishes and bake fifty pies, then head to school. His next job was with the university's Foundation Maintenance Department repairing and maintaining HVAC units and other facilities on campus including the dish washing area of the cafeteria where Burt had to replace the metal ball bearings on a conveyor belt roller. Burt had to replace them every month because the area was steam cleaned, which would remove the seals and dry out the lubrication causing the bearings to seize. It was costly for the school and time consuming.

Then, in a pattern he would repeat throughout his career, Burt came up with a unique solution to the problem. While learning to work on various tools in the engineering department, including a lathe, he had seen some work done with hardwoods impregnated with an oil preservative that acted as a lubricant. So he decided to take two four-inch samples of the special hardwood, lathe them into simple wood plugs that would replace the metal ball bearings on the heaviest-loaded conveyor roller. He did not tell his bosses, afraid they would either block him from doing it or simply sack him. The wood bearings worked to perfection and did not seize or fail for the duration of his employment. This turned out to be a watershed event in his young life, giving him the courage and confidence to think independently and employ radical, but simple, designs to achieve his goals.

His bearing fix exceeded his expectations. In 1987 Burt delivered the commencement address at CalPoly and received an honorary doctorate degree. During his visit, school officials took him on a tour of the campus which had changed considerably over the years. They wanted to show off the new cafeteria, but Burt demanded to see the old one. The surprised officials were stunned when he crawled under the counter to inspect that old conveyor roller, and there it was—the old wooden bearings were still working thirty-five years later!

At CalPoly Burt immersed himself in his aeronautical engineering studies. In 1964 he designed his first model with a canard configuration, assigning FX 935 as its tail number. This was a fun play on the tail number of the newest secret aircraft rolled out for the public by Lockheed's Skunk Works, the Kelly Johnson A11 subsequently known as the SR 71 Blackbird. Its tail number was FX 934. Little did

Burt know how closely he would follow in the footsteps of one of his heroes, a legendary aircraft designer and pioneer.

Burt, only a junior at CalPoly, was already thinking outside the box, placing his engine at the tail. "I figured a front engine, by blowing on the canard, would provide a big [upward] pitch change . . . so I mounted the engine high on the back to offset the effect." He built the model but was also beginning to think about building his own airplane. He built his own wind tunnel—on the rooftop of his Dodge Dart—where he would test a large scaled model of what would subsequently become Burt's first plane, the VariViggen.

In August 1962, Burt's first child, Jeffrey Albert Rutan, was born. The family moved to a rented house in San Luis Obispo, California. Despite all the obligations the young father had, and the monumental work load he carried, Burt managed to get excellent grades.

By the time he completed his junior year, he had qualified to attend the Space Technology Summer Camp held at Jet Propulsion Laboratory where the students would be immersed in the latest technology. The camp brought out the best and brightest from top colleges like Cal Tech, MIT and Stanford, and it gave him an opportunity to see where he stood in comparison. He decided they were smarter in theoretical subjects, but did not have a clue how to design anything. "I was buoyed," he said, recognizing that he was "one hundred times better prepared" for practical aeronautical engineering.

AIR FORCE FLIGHT TEST ENGINEER

In February and March 1965, companies and other organizations, including the U.S. Air Force, came to CalPoly to recruit and interview graduating engineering students. Two students who had graduated a year earlier and were now working at Edwards Air Force Base steered him to the Air Force by telling him how much fun they were having in flight test engineering. And "fun" has been a key word in Burt's lexicon—he wanted to do things that were "fun" and this

Figure 8   Edwards Air Force Base. US Air Force.

motif continued throughout his career. They got him excited about the prospects of working there. After a short spell of contemplating a job with Mattel Toys—"they wouldn't show me their R&D outfit because it was too secret"—he settled on Edwards as his top choice for the first phase of his career.

Burt graduated from CalPoly in 1965 placing third in his class. He went to Edwards and talked to a civil servant who would not even give him a tour of the base, but with two friends there pulling for him the Air Force hired him as a government employee with a GS-7 rating and an annual salary of $7,070. He could have gotten more money from some of the major private aeronautical companies, but he was following his passion.

Burt sought a place to live in the nearby city of Lancaster, founded in the 1870s as a water spot for the Southern Pacific Railroad on the route between San Francisco and Los Angeles. In 1965, when Burt moved there, it was an unincorporated city sitting at the upper edge of the Mojave desert in what was called the Antelope Valley—where no one had ever spied an antelope. The city of mostly single-level bungalows had little to attract residents other than its proximity to Edwards Air Force Base and the blaze of golden poppies that carpet the foothills each Spring. Burt leased a house for his family, which by August 30, 1965, had grown to four with the birth of his daughter Dawn.

His first assignment at Edwards was the Ling-Temco-Vought XC-142A, a vertical take-off and landing transport experimental airplane that never made it into production. Delivered to Edwards in September 1965, the XC-142A was a complicated piece of equipment with a tilt-wing, four huge propellers, and a tail propeller for pitch control in hover mode. It was similar to the tilt-rotor Osprey, but had a larger payload, and faster by one-hundred knots with twice the range. Its major deficit was that the propellers generated an excessive whirlwind of dirt, rocks and gravel.

The second year out of college Burt spent most of his time in El Centro, California, in the middle of the Colorado Desert bioregion,

Figure 9   Ling-Temco-Vought XC-142A. NASA.

just across the border from Mexicali, Mexico. Summer temperatures average well above 100 degrees and the rainfall can be measured with a tablespoon. His posting had much to do with the war in Viet Nam. In April 1967, the first offensive against the American base at Khe Sanh started when forces from the People's Army of Viet Nam encircled the base. Supplies had to be airlifted to Khe Sanh. It was impossible to resupply the base by ground transport. Burt's assignment was to engage in flight testing of low level aero-delivery by C-130 cargo planes. Sitting in the aft section of the C-130, Burt served as the flight test engineer working with different load configurations, dropping payloads of 35,000 or 45,000 pounds in low-level flights, causing abrupt pitch changes in the aircraft. "It was exciting," he said, and dangerous.

El Centro was not a garden spot and most civilian and military personnel would do anything to avoid it, but for Burt it had other benefits. "I ended up liking it more and more because my bosses were gone . . . I made per diem and hazard pay, flying almost every day. . .I was a youngster in hog heaven . . . just a year after college and I'm running the flight test program. It was pretty heady stuff." His closest boss was 210 miles away.

For the first four months of his tenure in El Centro, Burt's family stayed in Lancaster because the program was regarded by the military as temporary duty. It was not supposed to last more than a month or two and Burt was not given a permanent change of station. Finally, he rented a nice apartment in El Centro and brought his family, financing the move in part through his temporary duty benefits. The "temporary duty" lasted fourteen months before Burt and family returned to Edwards and their home in Lancaster.

In 1968 Burt also did some evaluation of the Navy's A-7 Corsair, a carrier-based subsonic light attack aircraft, but his biggest coup and major accomplishment was the work he did on the McDonnell Douglas F4 Phantom, a large two-seat, twin-engine, supersonic jet, the principal fighter employed in Viet Nam. The Air Force had lost approximately sixty F-4s, not to enemy fire or combat, but to departure loss of control and spins. The Navy had lost a similar number of planes for the same reasons. The F-4E program at Edwards was designed to be a Category II Stability and Control program, known as "sugar and cream" by flight test engineers. Burt was lead flight test engineer for the program and became a top expert on the stability and control issues of the jet. Working with Major Jerry Gentry, the test pilot, Burt would sit in the back of the F-4 as they tried various configurations of bombs, missiles, and payloads, often asymmetrical, and learned that some of the emergency procedures set forth in the craft's flight manual did not work.

The Air Force and Navy shunned spin test programs, believing they would lead to the craft's destruction and possible injury or death to the test pilots. Burt never received approval for a classic spin test

Figure 10 F-4 Phantom. US Air Force.

program, where intentional spins are done. The new program was titled Stalls and Near Stall Evaluations. However, Burt and Major Gentry found themselves in a hundred spins during the program - all were inadvertent, while testing stalls with a huge matrix of flight conditions and external bomb loads. And in one flight, Major Gentry and Burt were flying an F4E loaded asymmetrically with bombs, when it suddenly went into a flat spin at thirty-seven thousand feet. They lost twenty-thousand feet before the spin recovery parachute deployed and let them recover at seven thousand feet, a terrifying descent for Burt. As a result of these tests, Burt and Gentry established a procedure for more reliable recovery for all types of spin except the flat spin. They had discovered many important things about the fighter's flight dynamics and it led to major revisions in all aspects of stability and control procedures for the craft. Burt's work resulted in finding the right procedure to avoid a large number of the F4's historic losses.

At a meeting with four-star U.S. Air Force General William Momyer and two other generals, Burt, a lowly government employee, now with a GS-8 or GS-9 rating, who was not expected to say anything, suddenly got an inspiration and abruptly suggested that instead of giving F-4 pilots a piece of paper describing spin-recovery procedures, basically an addendum to the F-4's flight manual, that he and Major Gentry should make a personal presentation to all Air Force F4 pilots, show them films, explain what they had learned from the testing program, and be available to answer all questions. "It would save American lives," Burt told the surprised General. Momyer instantly responded, "That's a great idea!" and ordered the implementation of this proposal around the globe wherever F4s were stationed. Burt and Major Gentry flew to Washington D.C. and hand carried visa applications for nine different countries through embassy row. "We

Figure 11   Burt Rutan third from right with F-4 Flight Test Team. Courtesy of Burt Rutan.

briefed every [American] Air Force F4 pilot in the world, with trips as far west as Thailand and as far east as Turkey, forty-eight briefings in all," Burt said.

Not all was well on the domestic front. Burt was working long hours and weekends and spending much of his spare time on designing and building the VariViggen. In 1969 Judy abruptly pulled up stakes and left for Texas with the two kids. She was upset with him for many reasons, some not of his own doing. She was very religious; he was not. She was staunchly opposed to the Vietnam war and disliked the fact that he was doing war-related work with the Air Force. She also detested his brother Dick, an Air Force fighter pilot flying combat missions over there. Judy did not want Jeff or Dawn to have anything to do with Burt. She remarried and changed the children's last name without seeking Burt's approval. Judy moved to Texas, Ohio, and Idaho, in an irrational effort to keep the kids away from him. She even refused to accept child support from Burt who only saw his children a few times in Amarillo, Texas. Years later Burt flew his VariViggen to Burley, Idaho, and spent a few hours with them. He could not even be with them in a hotel or at night. Uninvited, he attended Jeff's high school graduation, but was subsequently reunited with his children after they left Judy's household.

Jeff recalled the traumatic period. "My mom and dad were divorced when I was seven. I was effectively kept away from my dad for most of my growing up years. . . but who I was and who I am was not so easily severed. As soon as I was on my own, I reconnected with my paternal grandparents and through them became reacquainted with my dad. I found him to be very different from how he had been represented to me. Although he was very much absorbed in his work, he still maintained a deep and abiding love for me and Dawn."

After graduating from high school Jeff changed his last name back to Rutan. "He also influenced my career path indelibly by giving me his first Apple computer in 1982," Jeff said, "along with the insight: 'Anything you can imagine this machine doing—you can make it do.'" Dawn and Jeff have maintained a very close relationship with Burt.

In 1971, Burt spent nearly five months at McDonnell Douglas's flight test center in St. Louis, Missouri, working on the F4 and developing flight test planning for the new F-15 Eagle, a twin-engine, all-weather tactical fighter that was schedule for first flights in 1972. At that facility he met Carolyn Weaver, a divorcee with two daughters who was a computer programmer at the center. They fell in love and Burt married her in St. Louis. He had left Lancaster as a bachelor and returned to Lancaster as the head of a family of four. To accommodate his new brood in the house he had rented, he had to evict his surprised roommates. Burt was worried, though. He didn't want Carolyn to see what he regarded as the "ugly desert," so he drove the mountainous route through Alpine-like Wrightwood, had dinner overlooking the desert thousands of feet below, then drove into town at night. "I didn't want her to have a bad impression." It was only a temporary fix, ending the following morning.

During his stay in St. Louis in 1971, Burt built a remote control version of the VariViggen and discovered that it would not fly; it would have to undergo various changes before he would attempt flight in his already built full-scale version of the craft.

SHORT STAY WITH BEDE AIRCRAFT CORPORATION AND THE VARIVIGGEN

Jim Bede, founder of Bede Aircraft Corporation, was the largest manufacturer of homebuilt kits in the United States. Plans and kits for the BD-4, a conventional high-wing cantilevered monoplane, were selling well and he was advertising his next generation, the BD-5, a small one-seater that some said resembled a micro fighter plane. The prototype had made a brief flight in September 1971, with a snowmobile engine, but the V-tail and other dynamics proved to be unstable. Nevertheless, Bede Aircraft Corporation was already taking $200 deposits—to preserve a place in line for the kits. Jim Bede claimed it could be easily built in anyone's garage and would fly twice as fast as a Cessna 150.

Though not privy to the BD-5 prototype's earlier problems, Burt suspected the airplane would be unstable; he was not a big fan of the plane. But he was interested in how Bede's kit was put together so he sent a deposit toward the purchase of the kit. Burt had a preliminary design in place for his own plane, one he initially called the MiniViggen, and had purchased the basic nuts and bolts to put it together, including the glue and the plywood. But he had to scrounge up other parts like the canopy of a sailplane. Bede had put an entire kit together, and using economies of scale and large purchase orders could reduce the price for the consumer. Burt felt he could use many of Bede's components: the fuselage, engine, drive shaft, propeller, the canopy, instruments, and landing gear. Burt's objective was to go into the homebuilt business and sell a kit and plans for a very low price. The box would come with some components, but page one of the plans would essentially say: "Step one, buy a BD-5 kit; step two take everything in this box and build a MiniViggen." Burt knew Jim Bede would not mind because every sale of Burt's MiniViggen kit would also result in a Bede sale of a BD-5 kit.

In late 1971, during a U.S.A. tour to demonstrate the BD-4, Jim Bede met Burt and offered him a job as his test pilot. Burt felt this was an opportunity to work with the top expert in homebuilt kits and thought it would be "as much fun as what I was doing in my garage." However, Burt explained that he was not a test pilot and that Bede should instead hire him as director of testing and design of the Bede Flight Testing Center, a position Burt felt Bede sorely needed. Once hired, he would find the right test pilot for the job. Burt also made it clear to Bede that he would not take a pay cut. Moreover, Burt told Bede that he would continue to work on his VariViggen project. "I wasn't thinking of becoming an entrepreneur…I just wanted to have fun."

Burt expected the work to last six to eight months, so in March 1972, he took what he thought would be a "sabbatical" from the Air Force. He had accumulated a significant stockpile of sick leave, and if he returned within a year would retain credit for all that sick leave. He was very excited about building the VariViggen and learning about homebuilt kits from Bede.

Within just a few months of having returned to Mojave with his new family, Burt was now discussing with Carolyn plans to get back on the road, this time bound for Kansas. He sold his place in line to purchase the BD-5 kit and in March the Rutans were heading back East. The VariViggen, with the outboard wings removed, was tucked into the moving van.

Bede's test facilities were in Newton, Kansas, and the Rutans rented a house in Valley Center just north of Wichita. When Burt showed up at the Bede Flight Test Center, the head of personnel was not aware of Burt's hiring. Apparently Bede had forgotten to mention it. The manager asked Burt "How much do I pay you?" and when

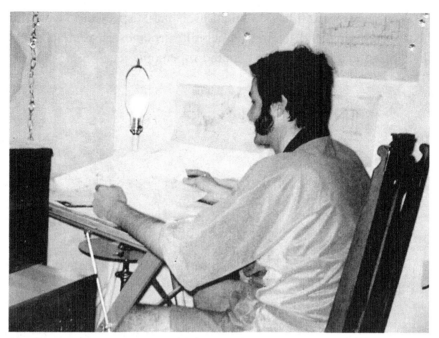

Figure 12 Burt working on the VariViggen plans in 1972. Courtesy of Burt Rutan.

Burt told him $18,000 a year, the man's face paled—nobody got paid that much at Bede. Burt showed him the signed letter from Bede and simply walked in and told the employees, "I'm the new boss." Burt felt the people Bede had hired were not the best at design protocol or development and he was prepared to do whatever was necessary to get the BD-5 project on track and moving forward. By the end of 1972, Bede had received deposits on approximately four-thousand kits.

Using Bede's shop facilities at the Bede Flight Test Center, Burt continued to work on the VariViggen. In April he got the engine running and started low speed taxi tests. A month later the proof-of-concept prototype, N27VV, Model 27, made its first flight, the 27 referring to the twenty-seventh modification of his original design. Burt flew the VariViggen to many airshows, demonstrating its unique characteristics and drumming up interest. The work on the

VariViggen was exciting. "I found as I had suspected," he wrote, "that developing and testing homebuilt airplanes is as much of a challenge and a lot more fun than the supersonic jets!"

Figure 13   Burt Rutan and stepdaughter Jetta in the VariViggen proof of concept. Courtesy of Burt Rutan.

In July, Burt flew the VariViggen to the EAA Oshkosh air show. The VariViggen must have seemed like an ethereal alien landing. Spectators were stunned by it. According to Jack Cox, author and former editor of *Sport Aviation*, "EAAers puzzled over the airplane's unfamiliar delta wing/canard configuration, but frequent flight demonstrations allayed any fears that this was some sort of far-out, dangerous airplane."

By late 1973, after nearly two years of enjoying flying his VariViggen, Burt started contemplating a future life as an entrepreneur and to give others an opportunity to enjoy the VariViggen experience. He decided to target only experienced or capable homebuilders, those who could build a complex airplane from a relatively simple set of plans. He would market the cursory plan set for $27. The customer would buy the parts and hardware necessary to complete the airplane.

To sell VariViggen plans while still at Bede, Burt formed Rutan Air Factory (RAF) as a sole proprietorship in 1973 and focused on completing development of the craft. Articles about the VariViggen began to appear in various aviation magazines and potential customers were lining up to buy plans for this novel aircraft. In the August issue of *Sport Aviation*, an article describing the VariViggen's performance characteristics appeared; it would be the first of many articles about Rutan aircraft that would appear in the next three-plus decades.

At the same time, Burt was working on the development of Bede Aircraft Corporation's BD-5J a small jet that could fly at three-hundred miles per hour. Burt was the principle designer of all the modifications to convert a propeller-driven BD-5A/B into the jet BD5J and he was enjoying the responsibility it entailed. The prototype jet made its first flight in 1973.

Meanwhile, the prop BD-5A/B had undergone four or five iterations as various problems arose, and it looked as if it would finally become an easy airplane to fly with good flying qualities. However, its two-stroke engine continued to have reliability problems. Burt was also becoming uncomfortable with the direction Bede's business was taking. Bede knew he might lose money on the kits, but expected to make it up on peripherals such as avionics, the way he believed Beech Aircraft and Cessna did it. When Bede's business began to fail, Bede decided to concentrate on developing a factory-built certified airplane (the BD-5D), with the certification being done in New Zealand to avoid what Bede believed was an over-aggressive U.S. certification process. Bede felt this would save his organization. Burt did not think it was a viable plan. Bede began collecting deposits for what Burt called "a certified plane that did not exist, and for a prototype that wasn't flying so well." These deposits allowed Bede to continue to buy parts for his ongoing kit business, but he was unable to secure all the parts needed for a complete BD-5 kit. Instead, he sent sub-kits, the first containing some parts, like the tail assembly, the next with other parts as they became available. In August 1974, one buyer writing a letter to *Sport Aviation* magazine, complained, "Maybe one day Bede will deliver all the components to build a complete plane—but when? At this point, I'd just like my money back." Bede responded that buyers would receive their kits, but was unable to deliver completed BD-5 kits before going into receivership. However, a number of BD-5s and BD-5Js have been built and are still flying today.

Figure 14 Bede Aircraft Corporation BD-5J, World's Smallest Jet. Courtesy Anheuser-Busch InBev.

RUTAN AIRCRAFT FACTORY YEARS

Burt did not want the problems Bede Aircraft Corp. was encountering to hamper his career. He had two choices: return to the Air Force or devote his full attention to RAF. He opted for the latter, believing success was possible if one had good ethics and a product people would buy. Moreover, based on the reception he had received at Oshkosh in the prior two years, with strong demand for plans for the VariViggen, he felt confident about his entrepreneurial prospects. "I borrowed an old Ercoupe to scout out where to move to. I needed a home for the family of four, a hangar for the VariViggen, and a shop for RAF big enough to build planes. I started at Brown field at the Mexican border and hopped to a dozen airports working north; when I arrived at Mojave, I finally found a place I could afford. That is why I chose Mojave. Also, if RAF failed, Mojave was a short twenty-minute drive to Edwards AFB where I knew I could get a job." Burt got a $15,000 loan from Pop and leased a World War II building at Mojave Airport. Building 13, the Spartan-like facility was primitive at best.

Burt then returned to Kansas to "gather my family," he recounted. "The trip from Kansas to Mojave was very interesting. Carolyn drove the Dodge station wagon and I flew the VariViggen, meeting up for lunch and for the several overnight motel stays."

By February 1975, there were 150 VariViggens under construction and many more plans sold, however, Burt knew he could improve upon the VariViggen. In 1974 he had begun to draw plans for a new craft, the VariEze ("very easy"), a two-place VW-engine-powered airplane built entirely out of composites—foam and fiberglass—a

Figure 15 Mojave Airport. US Air Force.

virtually stall- and spin-free aircraft. While at Bede, Burt had built a fiberglass-skin and solid-foam elevator and thought he could employ the same materials to build a complete composite airplane—the genesis of a new line of aircraft. He saw composites as the future. "I knew that a metal airplane and a wooden airplane were very work-intensive and took a lot of time," he told *The New York Times*. "I had built both. The VariViggen was a wooden airplane with the outer wings built out of metal. I did that so I could learn how to build metal airplanes. The VariEze was unique at that time in that it was a fiberglass airplane done without female molds."

The proof of concept VariEze, Model 31, made its maiden flight on May 21, 1975. Burt first demonstrated the VariEze at the Hollister Air Show; unfortunately there were few spectators in attendance. Burt subsequently announced in *Sport Aviation* that the VariEze "demonstrated 70 miles per gallon with two people aboard" and "would be available to homebuilders." The real unveiling took place two months later, on July 31, when Dick Rutan landed the VariEze on the Oshkosh runway before a crush of spectators. Jack Cox described it in *Sport Aviation* magazine: "An audible gasp arose from the crowd at the sight of the VariEze. . . I've never seen a more dramatic entrance." But Burt and Dick had a more stirring plan in mind for the airshow: Dick would fly the VariEze and break the closed course world distance record for airplanes weighing less than five-hundred kilograms. And he did it on August 4, with Burt following in the VariViggen. Dick took off from Runway 18 at Oshkosh and flew 1,638 miles in thirteen hours, eight minutes and forty-five seconds.

Burt was careful; he wasn't ready to sell the VariEze until he could work out several design issues he encountered in the flight test program, including one relating to the VW engine. He decided not to put out plans for the VariEze until he had redesigned the plane, replacing the VW engine with a Continental O-200 engine, employing ailerons on the wings, and incorporating other changes. People were sending him money to be first in line for the plans, but Burt returned the money with the Bede experience in mind. He wouldn't accept money until he was ready to deliver. "Something I sell has to be flight tested thoroughly. I don't sell them something that I'm going to do next year," he said.

On March 14, 1976, the new larger VariEze, Model 33, took off for its first flight. And three months later, after he completed the flight tests and signed off on the final plans, he was ready to sell plans and kits. A tidal wave of orders scaled the gates of Building 13.

Instead of using standard blueprints for his VariEze kits, Burt took a lesson from Simplicity dress patterns: He defined each step in building the plane, and showed a simple sketch demonstrating how to complete that step. Once completed, the builder would check it off, and move on to the next step. "The idea was to make it bulletproof. People could not leave things out or make mistakes," Burt said. "And it proved very successful." Generating a quarterly newsletter that described problems people encountered in building the kits or flying the planes helped make the VariEze successful.

Figure 16 Three of Burt Rutan's early airplanes (top to bottom) VariEze, VariViggen and LongEZ. Courtesy of Burt Rutan.

To meet the anticipated demand for parts with so many orders, Burt needed to establish reliable and fairly priced sources for the hardware and structural components. He decided to employ two companies to provide completed kits, knowing that healthy competition between the two would assure kit builders a fair price for the kit. He selected Aircraft Spruce & Specialty Company in Fullerton, California, and Wicks Aircraft Supplies in Illinois to supply the kits. Aircraft Spruce and Wicks Aircraft would ship the kits directly to the buyer and pay RAF a 7 percent royalty on each kit sold. He also arranged for Ken Brock Manufacturing in Stanton, California, to supply machined and welded parts for the plane. Not all customers used these vendors; they could take the bill of materials and scrounge for the parts elsewhere. This sales program afforded many benefits to a young and emerging company, and fit well with Burt's motto: keep it simple and efficient. He was sedulously avoiding the problems that sink nascent enterprises: high costs associated with buying, warehousing and shipping inventory, debt, and collecting accounts receivables.

With business booming, and reputation for his state-of-the-art designs growing, demand for Burt's services blossomed. Tom Jewett and Gene Sheehan wanted to design a plane that would provide "more flying enjoyment for less money." In 1977, they asked Burt to help them design a single-seat airplane with a canard configuration—the canard would have nearly the same area as the wings—and built with a minimal number of composite components. In what would become a characteristic of all the Rutan designs and project implementation, the first plane was a proof of concept and the flight of the newly-designed craft, the Quickie, took place in August, just a few months after Rutan first drew pen to paper. After a few design alterations, The Quickie, in its final configuration, took to the skies on November 17. The following year, Jewett and Sheehan formed the Quickie Aircraft Corporation in Mojave, near RAF, and flew the Quickie to Oshkosh where it garnered considerable attention and received an award for the Outstanding New Design. Sales of the Quickie kit were brisk and about three thousand Quickie sets were sold.

Other projects were on the RAF drawing board including the AD-1. The story behind the AD-1, a skew-wing jet designed by Burt for the National Aeronautics and Space Administration (NASA), is as unique as the craft itself. It was Burt's first experience with

NASA. The story begins with Dick Fisher, a NASA engineer who graduated from CalPoly a year ahead of Burt. Stationed at NASA's Dryden Flight Research Center at Edwards Air Force Base, Fisher had been involved with NASA's attempt to develop a research airplane that would use the skew-wing configuration in transonic flight. The skew-wing, also known as the scissors- or oblique-wing, would remain in the standard vertical T-like position for better lift and control during takeoff and slow flight, but at higher speeds the wing would rotate into an asymmetrical position resembling slightly ajar scissors when compared to the fuselage.

Figure 17   AD-1 Skew-Wing Jet. NASA.

Developing the transonic version of such a plane was deemed to be a complex and very expensive research project. Fisher thought a manned subsonic plane would show the take off , landing and slow-speed capabilities of the jet. Having seen Burt build the VariEze in three-and-a-half months, he suggested that Burt submit an unsolic-ited feasibility study to NASA for the design of a skew-wing sub-sonic plane that NASA could test.

Burt had seen drawings of a Boeing skew-wing transonic airliner that never made it off the drafting table. Burt scaled it down to a single pilot, designed a larger tail and submitted a two-page proposal to perform a feasibility study on whether the plane could be built by RAF. NASA accepted his proposal, priced at $960. Doing something for NASA was "a feather in my cap," Burt recalled.

The feasibility study concluded that a 15 percent scaled flying model of the Boeing transonic airliner could be built for a single pilot to fly. It would be a subsonic, twin-engine jet with fixed gear. Burt next submitted a bid to NASA to make drawings for $11,500. It was "good money" since he didn't think it would take him more than six to eight months to complete the drawings. NASA, unaccustomed to such small change, thought he had slipped the decimal into the wrong column and even called him to advise him of his mistake. Burt told them the price was, indeed, $11,500.

Burt finished and delivered the drawings to NASA and, per government regulations, NASA put it out for competitive bidding. They sent Burt a bid package, a sheaf of documents several inches thick. Burt reviewed the regulations and realized RAF could not comply with several conditions—drafted with larger companies in mind. The drawings for a plane built of cut foam, wire, fiberglass contact, akin to the VariEze, was something companies like Boeing, Lockheed and others, were probably stunned to see. If they did not laugh, they certainly did not bid.

Burt "got cold feet" about the job but talked to his friend Herb Iverson of Ames Industrial Co., of Bohemia, New York, which provided the jet engines for the BD-5J when Burt worked on the Bede Aircraft project. Ames met all the NASA requirements and regulations. Ames agreed to submit a bid if Burt would help them build the plane.

NASA got only one bid—from Ames Industrial—to deliver a ready-to-fly airplane for $218,000. Every contract above $100,000 had to be approved by NASA headquarters in Washington and it was quickly ratified. Burt did not anticipate any major problems; as he put it, he had designed the aircraft that would be "VariEze" to build.

NASA's subsequent review of progress on the signed contract probably cost the government agency more than the contract price itself, with official visits to Ames, astronaut test pilots arriving in

F-104 fighters to see the AD-1 under construction, and for accountants to audit the fixed-price contract. And one month before Ames was ready to deliver the AD-1 to Dryden, the Dryden media center submitted a draft press release to NASA's Washington headquarters for review. Washington responded essentially with "what the heck is this?" Based on the low price they thought they had approved a model airplane. Although they had approved the contract they did not realize it was for a manned craft; how could a piloted jet aircraft be built for only $218,000, they wanted to know. The AD-1 was delivered to Dryden in February 1979, and made its maiden flight on December 21 of that year. Its last flight was at the Oshkosh airshow, where it thrilled the crowd making passes with the wings rotated to the full sixty-degrees skew. It was subsequently delivered to the Hiller Aviation Museum where it now resides.

Pug Piper, son of Bill Piper the founder of Piper Aircraft, approached Burt in 1977 to build a new all-composite airplane for Piper Aircraft Corp., a wholly-owned subsidiary of Bangor Punta. Piper said they would get the plane certified and put it into production, but Burt and Piper could not agree on how to work together. Certification would take six to ten years, and like another famous aviation pioneer before him, Jack Northrop, Burt was not interested in spending so much time on one airplane. Piper hired George Mead, who had previously worked for Burt and went ahead and built a new composite single-engine plane with a canard named the PAT-1. Aviation pundits nicknamed it the "Pug Mobile." The prototype later crashed during a NASA evaluation, killing Mead and two NASA engineers. The PAT-1 program was then cancelled.

Burt was facing a major dilemma: what to do after the VariEze. He wanted to make a plane for himself, a push-pull twin-engine craft with his signature canard configuration using the technologies he developed in the construction of the VariEze,. The Defiant, a nicely balanced plane with the safety of a twin, but more so, was born. One of the greatest dangers pilots can encounter in flying a twin-engine plane is to have an engine fail on departure, close to the ground. The plane will yaw wildly to the side of the dead engine and the pilot has to take immediate action to eliminate the yaw while maintaining a rate of climb on the remaining engine. Burt was seeking to develop a twin-engine plane that would be essentially stall- and spin-free. If an engine failed, the pilot would just continue to fly the airplane with lower performance. "It was a wonderful airplane, stall free, a four-seater with a huge payload . . . it turned out to be much better than I thought it would be," Burt said.

The proof of concept model of the Defiant made its first flight on June 30, 1978. The Defiant, with an eleven-hundred-nautical mile range, burning 11.7 gallons per engine per hour, with a maximum speed of 188 knots, was the best four-seat twin-engine plane of comparable size on the market—and the safest.

"I was a glutton for simplicity," Burt acknowledged. The Defiant even had fixed-pitched propellers, which led to its only deficiency: without the extra drag from the idled constant-speed propellers, the pilot could not make steep approaches without building up speed. Burt did not have detailed plans or construction photos for the plane since he had not planned on making it into a kit. Burt designed the Defiant to show how a twin-engine, push-pull craft could be made so simple to fly that the pilot would not have to worry about yaw or rate of climb. Although Burt thought it was one of his finest planes, he did not want to go through the tasks of certification or production. "I chose instead to go ahead with many more research airplanes," he said. "My heart was in the research area, not production." Nevertheless, he created plans for the craft as a homebuilt and a score or more were constructed. The Defiant prototype, like the AD-1, now resides at the Hiller Aviation Museum in San Carlos.

The success of the VariEze may have also led to marital discord. Carolyn was deathly afraid of potential lawsuits arising from an accident in one of the RAF homebuilts, and that they would lose everything they had worked so hard to achieve. Unable to take the stress, or for Burt to mitigate it, the marriage unraveled and Carolyn left in

1978. Burt and his current wife, Tonya, still socialize with Carolyn and occasionally with Judy. We "enjoy each other's company," he mused.

Although more than three thousand VariEze kits had been sold by the end of 1979, Burt felt he could improve on the design and make a better plane. And in June 1979, the prototype of the LongEZ made its first flight. With a range of sixteen-hundred miles at maximum cruise speed or more than two-thousand miles at economy cruise speed, the LongEZ, a two-seater like the VariEze but larger and with better aerodynamic capabilities, became a favorite with the homebuilt community. Its range was so extensive, especially if an additional fuel tank was inserted in lieu of the second seat, that in 1997 Burt's brother, Dick, and Mike Melvill flew their LongEZs around the globe, mostly over oceans of the Southern Hemisphere, stopping in exotic spots like Pitcairn Island, Easter Island and cities in Australia and South Africa. Burt didn't think flying over so much water in a single-engine plane was a good idea, but the flights ended successfully. The LongEZ had an excellent reputation; however, one LongEZ brought about unwanted publicity—it was the airplane in which singer John Denver died a few months after Melvill and Dick had completed the round-the-world flight. The crash had nothing to do with the plane's aerodynamics or design, according to the National Transportation Safety Board. The builder of that LongEZ changed the fuel valve configuration and Denver only had a thirty-minutes check ride in that plane. Unable to work the fuel valve properly he ran out of fuel and crashed into the Pacific Ocean, only 150 yards from the rocky shore, near Pacific Grove, California.

Burt incorporated RAF in early 1980. General aviation aircraft manufacturers in general were not faring well. Facing soaring litigation and insurance costs, the production of general aviation aircraft fell dramatically, from eighteen-thousand planes in 1978 to just nine-hundred in 1993. Piper Aircraft Corporation filed for bankruptcy and Cessna Aircraft Company ceased producing single-engine planes in 1986. The industry was nearing the point of utter collapse. The homebuilt market was not impervious to litigation or rising insurance; Burt would suffer through twelve lawsuits. Interestingly, John Denver's estate filed a wrongful death lawsuit against the airplane's builder and several component supplies, but the suit did not involve Burt.

He did not carry any liability insurance and, most of the time, after plaintiffs' counsel discovered that his pockets were not deep, the lawsuits mystically evaporated. If counsel demanded or expected a quick settlement, they were in for a surprise and quickly disabused of the notion—Burt was not easily cowed. He simply refused to settle. Only one of the lawsuits went to trial. It involved the death of a pilot and his passenger in a VariEze. The pilot was intoxicated, had forgotten to install one of the four bolts that attached the wing to the fuselage, and performed aerobatics in a plane that was not certified for such maneuvers. The passenger's estate brought a lawsuit against Burt, RAF and the estate of the deceased pilot. Somehow, plaintiff's counsel thought Burt should be held responsible. A long and protracted jury trial ensued. The jury sided with Burt and punished the plaintiff's counsel, but that's another story. Several members of the jury subsequently attended Burt's fly-in surprise birthday parties at Mojave.

SCALED COMPOSITES – THE BEGINNING

After conducting research development programs for NASA and Fairchild and design work for Beechcraft, Burt found that he preferred to do research work that did not involve supporting the individual homebuilder. Also, he didn't want to burden big research customers with the costs of consumer liability protection. Burt sought out Herb Iversen, his old friend who had supplied the BD-5 jet engines and who had built the AD-1. Together they teamed up and formed a new company, one that would not deal with the public. Scaled Composites was incorporated in early 1982 and got its seed money by selling a minority equity position to investors Howard Keck and Joe Scherzinger. These investors provided capital for the purchase of a building and to provide enough working capital for six months. It freed Burt to focus on designing new planes while operating debt free. Like Henry Ford, who disdained debt, Burt sedulously avoided it throughout his career. Burt retained a 51 percent ownership of the new corporation. Scaled was successful from inception, and Burt did not have to get any additional investment or borrow funds for operations.

RAF continued in business with several ongoing projects including the LongEZ. RAF had two loyal employees, Mike and Sally Melvill, who did not have any interest in moving to Scaled.. "I thought, well, I'm a young guy," Burt recalled, "and there's nothing else to do in Mojave; I can run both businesses. And the buildings were fifty feet apart." Burt continued to sell plans for the LongEZ for another three years, and RAF's doors remained open to support builders for nearly twenty years.

The biggest project at RAF involved Beech Aircraft Corp. a subsidiary of Raytheon. Seeking a new twin-engine model to replace its aging King Air line, Beech asked Burt and RAF to design concepts for what they called NGBA (Next-Generation Business Aircraft). To assure Burt that they would indeed be receptive to something revolutionary, Beech offered an artist's graphic, which looked like a scaled-up LongEZ. RAF responded with five or six different design concepts and Beech selected the one with the unique, sweeping canard, high-lift system. After Scaled Composites Inc. was formed in mid 1982, Burt assigned RAF's contract for the development of NGBA to Scaled. Later, after Lindon Blue was named president of Beech, he named the new design "Starship One."

In 1985, Mike and Sally formed a division of Scaled to do projects for Scaled using the RAF facility, and three years later they joined Burt as employees of Scaled.

To proceed with a new airplane materially different from any business or other commercial jet in service, on the market, and probably on any manufacturer's drawing board was a huge decision by the old Beech company. In many ways the Starship looked other-worldly without a tail, two turboprop engines in the rear, and tall winglets with rudders. Built mostly of fiberglass, the Scaled-built 85-percent-proof-of-concept prototype Starship made its first flight in August 1983. Beech president Blue introduced Starship 1 at the National Business Aviation Association (NBAA) in Dallas, Texas. The NBAA Convention News announced:

"The Starship was inspired by the configuration of the homebuilt LongEZ. Indeed, both airplanes came from the fertile mind of Burt Rutan, who was later named a v-p at Beech. Rutan's Starship performed a stunning flyby over the NBAA static display at Dallas Love field, stopping traffic and lowering jaws for a full 10-minute performance that rocked the aviation world."

Intended to fly one-hundred hours in test flights, which it did in only thirty-five days, the proof-of-concept prototype eventually accumulated more than five-hundred hours of flight testing. Beech built a number of Starships. *Air & Space* magazine noted that, "Twenty-five years after it was first conceived, the Beech model 2000 Starship is still a head-turner. . .While flying at 31,000 feet Starship pilot Bob Bass received a radio call from a U.S. Air Force jet that wanted to pull alongside." It was a $2 billion Northrop Grumman B-2 flying-wing bomber—its pilot wanted to take photographs of the Starship.

FIRST BLOCKBUSTER – THE VOYAGER

Burt's older brother, Dick, a Viet Nam war hero with more than three-hundred combat missions who had been shot down over North Vietnam and was also ejected from an F-100 after engine failure, left the Air Force in 1979 and went to work for RAF. Two years later he decided it was not tenable to work for his five-year-younger brother. Dick enjoyed flying Burt's planes, but he did not like Burt telling him what he could or could not do with the planes, like flying one of the single-engine airplanes on the deck of the Kern River Canyon, where, according to Burt, "one hiccup in the engine would leave the airplane and pilot in splinters." Dick, an exceptionally skilled pilot also performed aerobatics—loops and snap rolls—in Burt's planes which were not designed for aerobatics; they were designed for cross-country flying. "He was taking real big risks that I wouldn't take myself," Burt said. Dick loved to fly, but Burt was concerned that people would see Dick performing aerobatics and assume the planes were built to be flown that way, with potentially calamitous results. Burt felt Dick was not at risk of becoming a defendant in a lawsuit, but the designer was. The two brothers also had different business visions. Dick felt Burt was not taking advantage of a real business opportunity, selling kits instead of plans. On the other hand, Burt did not want the risks associated with manufacturing kits or the headaches inherent in dealing with inventory; he was satisfied simply getting his royalty on kits manufactured and sold by others.

Dick also wanted Burt to develop an aerobatic plane at RAF, but Burt would not go along with it—aerobatic planes had a high rate of accidents and the concomitant liability was extensive. Burt's passion was efficiency, not aerobatics. Unable to reconcile their differences, Dick left RAF in 1981, determined to go into the kit-building business. It was an amicable parting. Dick and his girlfriend, Jeana Yeager, decided to form a new company and called a dinner meeting at the Overpass Café in Mojave to ask Burt to design the plane—one that could conceivably compete with Burt's planes, something only a brother could ask. Instead, Burt suggested building something else that would tweak Dick's appetite: "How would you like to be the first person to fly around the world without stopping to refuel?" Burt asked. This would be a real record-breaking milestone.

Circumnavigating the globe without stopping or refueling was considered an impossible task at the time; no one was planning to pursue such an impossible dream because it would require doubling the old distance record (aviation records are normally set by smaller increments of 5 to 10 percent). Jim Bede had tried it, but failed. As far as anyone knew, the technology for such an undertaking did not exist. The farthest any craft had flown without refueling was an Air Force B-52 that held the long-distance record of nearly thirteen-thousand miles. The daunting and risky adventure Burt proposed appealed to Dick, and Burt quickly drew on a napkin a sketch of a plane he had been contemplating, one with a wingspan exceeding one-hundred feet. It was "not the classic napkin sketch of an inventor," Burt noted. Dick and Jeana wanted to complete construction of the plane in eight months, thinking that if Burt could build a VariEze in three-and-a-half months, building this craft in eight months was feasible.

Burt was motivated to become involved in the project by several factors. Creating a unique plane for such a mission, one that no one else would or could build or fly, would not generate any liability exposure. On the contrary, if successful, it would bring in a windfall of business for RAF and Scaled. Burt did not plan on building the whole craft. He thought he might build some section like the fuselage or the tail assembly; that Dick would put it out for bid and Burt would bid on some part of it. Accordingly, Burt did not do any more

Figure 18   Burt and Dick Rutan discussing the Voyager in 1984. Courtesy of Burt Rutan.

work on it, expecting Dick, once he had money in hand, to contract with others for final design and construction.

Dick expected that such an historic undertaking would make it fairly easy to raise the funds. It was not. Dick and Jeana spent one-and-a-half years trying to raise the money. Dick refused to take any funds from tobacco or liquor companies, including a $2 million offer from one concern, because he equated such firms with drug dealers. JVC, a large Japanese conglomerate offered to fund it, but placed time constraints on completing the mission. Fortunately, Burt talked Dick and Jeana out of signing that contract—it was not feasible and the time limits imposed by JVC were impossible to fulfill.

Dick had also approached several deep pockets including H. Ross Perot and Baron Hilton, but their attorneys were not sanguine about the venture; they could see their client's logo splashed on the tail of the craft as it ended up in the ocean. It was too risky for them. Even Burt was uncertain about its prospects; he had never designed anything like it with only the VariEze, AD-1, LongEZ, Starship and Grizzly under his belt.

Dick finally approached Burt and discussed the prospects of working together on developing the plane, aptly named Voyager by Dick. Burt had talked to their parents, and agreed to have RAF structure the program so that it could be done for a small sum of money. They would hire one person, with Dick and Jeana working without pay, and Burt, Mike and Sally Melvill, working on a best-effort basis to get materials donated. Pop and Irene provided Dick and Jeana with room and board to help mitigate their costs of living. There was no specific schedule set for completion.

It was a complex undertaking, and Burt had no idea whether it would work, whether the plane could circle the planet without refueling, a determination that could only be made after the craft was designed, built, and tested. There were many issues to address other than design and construction, from the kind of weather radar they would need, to long-range radio and other communication gear, and finding efficient engines and propellers that could measure up to the task.

Initially an RAF covert operation, the Voyager's structural parts were fabricated at the small RAF shop, and the parts were later assembled in six sections in the much larger Hangar 77, contributed to the venture by the Mojave Airport manager. Burt did all the detail design, aided by John Roncz who designed the airfoil shapes for the wing and the canard, and by Chuck Richie who detailed the landing gear parts. Burt called them "Roncz airfoils." The craft was constructed with what Burt called "junk engines" to test its performance.

Voyager was difficult to fly and, without a full load of fuel, susceptible to turbulence in conditions where other planes would fly smoothly. In turbulence the wings would flop up and down like wings of a bird, but unlike a bird's body, which remains stable and inert, the main fuselage of Voyager would oscillate up and down, whipped by the long and slender wings. This tendency made it extremely uncomfortable for the pilots. Chase and other planes flying near Voyager

Figure 19 Voyager. Courtesy of Burt Rutan.

would suddenly peal away when the wings began to arc. Dick asked Burt how far can the wings bend before snapping off. According to Dick, "Burt told me they would bend upwards over thirty feet before breaking." Burt, however, said, " I actually told him there would be bending relief when the tips touch each other, but that did not seem to sink in." Voyager was a slow craft, designed for endurance and safety, not comfort or speed, causing Dick to complain about the possibility of "bird strikes to the trailing edge" of the wings.

Voyager made its first flight on June 22, 1984. "The first flight was made at very light weight and in smooth air, with no turbulence," Burt said. "Dick was delighted with the flying qualities and judged the airplane as having 'good, mission capable' handling. However, as the test program proceeded we learned two new things that were both bad; at light weights, even in light turbulence, the wings would move up and down at large deflections—six to ten feet in light turbulence and a frightful fifteen to eighteen feet in moderate turbulence. The wing flapping got considerably less as fuel was added, especially if the fuel was added to the tip or outboard parts of the wing. But the bigger problem occurred at the very heavy weights; the weights Voyager would sustain for the first two days of its world flight. At those heavy weights Voyager would oscillate in pitch (most noticeable by wing flapping) even without turbulence. And worse yet, if the flapping was not countered by continuous pilot inputs it would get worse and would probably break the wing within five or six cycles. It could be dampened automatically by the autopilot but if the autopilot failed during the first two days the pilot would have a difficult job of flying it back to any remote airport."

Several times during the test program the test cards showed Dick and Jeana flying overnight, but they always landed before sunset. Nevertheless, they were determined to do it, and Dick flew it to Oshkosh a month later, though the flight was so turbulent and physically draining that upon landing in Salina, Kansas, to refuel, Dick was demonstrably upset. "I got out of the airplane," he recalled, "and I was so tired and disgusted, that this bloody thing had any chance of going around the world; I had to be physically restrained from punching a hole in the wing tank, draining the fuel out on the ground, lighting that damned thing on fire, taking my pilot's license out and throwing it into the fire and taking a train home."

After mid 1984, Dick and Jeana acquired Burt's share of the project and took over managing it. They made a deal with Continental for a liquid-cooled engine and with Bendix/King, a subsidiary of Allied-Signal, for avionics, all provided to them on consignment. They also managed to get a force of volunteers to work on the final construction of the Voyager.

In July 1984, Voyager made one long-distance, 11,600-mile, four-and-a-half-day flight off the California coast to test flying conditions and the plane's aerodynamic performance and stability. It was the first time they actually slept in the airplane, but Jenna fainted just after landing.

Still, it was touch and go. "Our own data said that the Voyager flight was probably not going to happen," Burt told Andy Meisler of the *New York Times*. "We had seven major failures in the three-hundred-forty hours the plane had flown, and we were planning a 225-hour single flight, almost all over oceans."

With so few test flights under their wings, one resulting in a dead-stick landing on a dry lake at Edwards Air Force Base, another in an sudden deep plunge when rain struck the canard, and four flights aborted earlier than planned due to the craft's rough handling in turbulent air, Dick and Jeana faced many unknowns. Burt worked with John Roncz, someone he considers a genius when it comes to airfoil design, to find a cure for the loss of lift due to the rain, but without any further flight tests in rainy conditions, they could not be absolutely certain that their airfoil fix would work.

RAF did not spend much money and Burt did not charge for his time. The labor costs to construct Voyager were less than the cost of materials. RAF, Burt and Dick did a lot of materials testing, while Dick came up with some novel ways to raise more money, such as naming someone a VIP—a Voyager Important Person—for a $100 donation with their name carried aboard the historic round-the-world flight.

Embarking on a voyage expected to last almost ten days, living in this tiny seven-and-a-half-foot-long torpedo-like capsule with about as much room as the cockpit of a glider or the interior of a Japanese capsule hotel room, would have been daunting for a single pilot, let alone two—only one could sit up at a time. Making matters worse, Dick and Jeana were now estranged, yet about to be cooped up together in this tiny cell for an extended length of time. Dick understood the rigors he was about to undertake and trained like a Zen-master and triathlete to get prepared physically and mentally for the arduous voyage.

At 8:01 a.m. on December 14, 1986, Voyager, resembling an airborne catamaran with long, thin delicate wings, began her take-off roll on the fifteen-thousand-foot runway at Edwards Air Force Base. Voyager had never been flown with full tanks—laden with over seven-thousand pounds of fuel tucked into the wings, twin-booms, and the fuselage. As Voyager gathered speed, its two engines at full throttle, Dick held the elevators in the down position for the takeoff roll to avoid a premature liftoff.

Pop, watching Voyager's takeoff described it: "Soon I saw an unexpected sight. Voyager was screaming closer. But both wing-tips seemed glued to the rough runway surface, and a white plume extended back in a vortex at each end. It couldn't be smoke; was it vaporized fuel? No? Oh, of course; it had to be the by-product of the wing itself being ground to a fine powder." The winglets scraped along eight-thousand feet of runway. The Voyager finally lifted off, its wings suddenly arcing upward, with only eight-hundred feet of the long runway remaining. It was eerily reminiscent of Charles Lindbergh's takeoff from Roosevelt Field on his historic solo across the Atlantic, where the fuel-laden *Spirit of St. Louis* barely cleared the trees and telephone wires at the end of the runway. As the Voyager slowly climbed west of Edwards and headed toward the Pacific Ocean, the winglets fell off together with the red and green navigation lights. Burt, Dick, Jeana and others at mission control determined that the loss of the winglets did not merit scrubbing the mission. A decision to abort the mission and have the plane land with full tanks was virtually inconceivable—it could not be done even with a pilot as skilled as Dick.

Ground control, manned round the clock, with Melvill doing the lion's share at night and Burt popping in from time to time during the day while working on the Starship and other projects at Scaled, tried desperately to deal with the exhausted and psychologically fragile pilots. At times Dick and Jeana refused to heed the advice of the mission's physician, and at other times sought his advice. There were times mission control knew to keep silent; at other times they had to intercede and talk to the exhausted voyagers.

As if this was not enough, Dick and Jeana had to endure constant engine noise exceeding 100 decibels, review revised flight plans sent by mission control every six hours as weather dictated, avoid bad weather or headwinds, including Typhoon Marge, maintain radio silence over Uganda (which refused entry into its air space),

Figure 20 Voyager during global flight – notice missing winglets on wing tips. Courtesy of Burt Rutan.

and get past Kenya which ordered them to land because they were violating Kenyan air space. Dick and Jeana had plenty of food and water for the duration of the flight, but they were risking their lives in the same way Lindbergh had risked his fifty-nine years earlier.

And during the last night, flying along the coast of Costa Rica with the U.S. just six hours away, a fuel transfer pump failed. The transfer pump was used to pump fuel from any of the eighteen fuel tanks into a feed tank that both engines used. Instead of replacing the pump, Dick had turned a valve to require the engine to draw fuel directly from a remote wing tank, not from the usual engine feed tank. This caused the rear cruise engine to fail due to low fuel pressure. It was pitch black outside and Dick was initially reluctant to start the front engine. He descended in a spiral, trying to keep the rear propeller wind-milling. After Melvill urged him to start the front engine, he did, and regained the nose-up attitude enough build up sufficient fuel pressure to restart the rear engine. After that frightening experience,

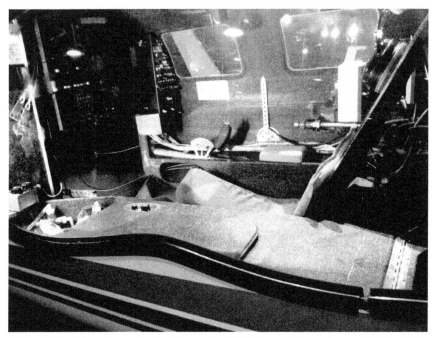

Figure 21 Voyager cockpit with room for only one pilot, manned 85% of the time by Dick Rutan. Author's Personal Collection.

Jeana got to work and replaced the failed transfer pump. The shaken crew decided to not shut down the front engine after that, so Voyager flew the last hours of the world flight with two engines running. This was less efficient; however, now that they knew they had enough fuel to get home it was a relief to again have a multi-engine airplane after flying nearly six days on one engine.

Few had the skills to do it; even fewer could have managed to pull it off. The hazards associated with round-the-world flights are well reflected by the death of such famous pilots as Wiley Post (with his passenger Will Rogers) and Amelia Earhart.

Running between Scaled and mission control, Burt was under extreme pressure, helping Shane and Melvill at ground control, working at Scaled, attending press conferences, checking weather reports, answering questions, providing answers and technical advice

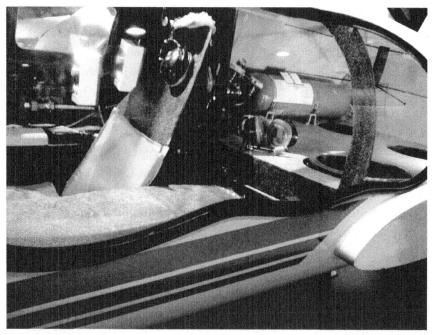

Figure 22 Voyager cockpit with small compartment in rear where only Jeana could fit (near the oxygen tank), but only lie down, in a curled, fetus-like position; she could not sit up. Author's Personal Collection.

on issues that arose. To add to his woes, during the week Pop was hospitalized—perhaps from the strain of the dangerous project—and Burt's daughter, Dawn, gave birth to her first child.

One of the most emotional moments for Burt took place as Voyager approached San Diego in the darkness near the end of the flight. Burt and Melvill were searching the skies in their plane, trying to find Voyager which only had a strobe light since its navigation lights were lost on take off. Mission Control was concerned about general aviation aircraft trying to converge on Voyager to eyewitness the historic event, so Burt and Melvill gave several false position reports in their radio transmissions. When they finally saw the strobe light, and had Dick turn it on and off to identify the plane, Burt and Melvill started to bawl, letting their long-held emotions flow freely. Voyager landed at Edwards at 8:06 a.m. on December 23, after covering 24,986 miles in nine days, three minutes and forty-four seconds, averaging 116 miles per hour, only nine miles per hour faster than Lindbergh's *Spirit of St. Louis*. They had only seventeen gallons of fuel left.

If the publicity surrounding Burt was substantial before Voyager, with more than ninety articles featuring RAF and Burt in magazines and on NBC's *Nightly News*, ABC's *Good Morning America*, *Omni Magazine*'s New Frontiers, *What's Up America*, and Frontiers of Flight—all occurring by June 1984, the Voyager flight put Burt on the front page of virtually every newspaper on the globe. And Burt was only getting started.

Time magazine said, "[T]he mission's undisputed star was Voyager, a distinctive, almost ethereal craft, whose shell weighs only 939 lbs …," a composite structure built of quarter-inch panels of paper honeycomb and graphite embedded in epoxy. The composite was one-fifth the weight of aluminum, the principal material used in construction of planes, and seven times stronger. Voyager became the first Burt Rutan-designed craft to find a home in the Smithsonian Air and Space Museum where it is displayed in the entry lobby.

1/5 wt -(Al   7x stronger

HEXCEL CORE
Carbon fiber + epoxy

X X X X X X X

Scaled and Regime Changes

RAF stopped selling plans in 1985, remaining open only to service those who had previously purchased plans or had built their craft. "[T]he bottom line was that both businesses were profitable, they were both something that I could easily support my family on, but one of them had a very high product liability exposure," Burt told *The New York Times*. "I still have these [RAF-designed] airplanes flying, and regardless of what happens to them—if they run into a mountain with a drunk pilot—there's still a risk that I could be sued for bad design. So I decided that I should cut off further exposure to product liability, and I stopped selling plans in June of '85."

Work on the Starship program was proceeding well. Jim Walsh, CEO of Beechcraft, was one of Burt's admirers and Burt respected Walsh's executive ability and vision. In 1985 Beech Aircraft Corp., with Raytheon's approval, offered to acquire Scaled Composites from Burt and his fellow investors and convert it into the Beech Advanced Design Center. Mainly because his strong relationship with Walsh, Burt and Scaled's principals agreed and the deal was consummated in June. Burt received a bonus for his work and innovation and the other investors made a very handsome profit from the sale of Scaled. Moreover, Walsh subsequently arranged some Beech stock options for key Scaled employees. For the first time in his life, Burt was liquid and financially healthy. And the first production-sized model of the Starship flew on February 15, 1986.

Burt had no interest in the production end of the business. "If I'd gone into manufacturing the Defiant in 1978," he said, "would I have done the Starship and the Voyager? Probably not. Would I have done America's Cup? No. Would we have our candy store? No way."

On a business trip to Beechcraft in Wichita in 1984, Burt met Margaret Rembleski, the daughter of a Beechcraft vice president, when her father included her in a business dinner at a fancy Wichita restaurant. They were married that year, but the marriage only lasted twenty months; she wanted kids and left in great haste when Burt learned he was unable to have more children. It was not a friendly parting. Burt described the 1986 divorce as "mean and expensive," and vowed never to marry again. But Burt was not destined for the bachelor life. In late 1986 Burt met Tonya Simone on a blind date set up by Dick's ex wife Geri and Tonya's mother. It took another seven years of being together before Burt proposed. They were married in 1993 at Tonya's mom's house. They've now been together for more than a quarter of a century and Burt says, "[S]he's the best partner I've had."

Figure 23   Beech Starship. Courtesy of Robert Scherer.

While Scaled was under the aegis of Beechcraft, Burt began the development of another project, a light attack turbofan jet fighter. In response to the U.S. Army's interest in the development of an anti-tank and anti-helicopter weapon, Burt suggested a new plane, but because it would be a fixed-wing craft, it came under the purview of the Air Force. When he heard nothing further from either branch, he "decided, heck it's not that expensive if we borrow an engine and a gun. We had a full ejection seat left over from the production Starship testing. So let's go build it and if it flies like we think it will, we can call up the Pentagon and say 'Hey, you guys want to evaluate this thing?'" So Scaled built the craft on spec without a government contract. Burt used engineers with down time to work on the project—in many ways it was like the old AD-1, he would go to the Pentagon and present an unsolicited jet fighter for evaluation. Like so many of Burt's designs, the Mud Fighter, now called Ares,

Figure 24   Burt working on design of Starship. Courtesy of Burt Rutan.

Figure 25   Ares. Courtesy of Burt Rutan.

had a unique appearance and characteristics, with a single jet engine inlet mounted on one side and angled outward but still maintaining center-line thrust, with a machine gun mounted on the other side firing along a groove, so the gun's exhaust remained far from the inlet and would not cause a flameout. It was a fast and exceptionally maneuverable plane with the same stall-proof qualities of the other early Rutan designs.

In 1987, Walsh left Beechcraft when he was passed over as chairman of Raytheon and moved to another public company, Wyman-Gordon, as president. Max Bleck, former president of Piper Aircraft Corp. succeeded Walsh at Beechcraft. Bleck was not a fan of Burt or the Starship and assailed the program from inception. "I tried to kill the airplane twice," Bleck said, once in 1987 and again four years later. Burt was unhappy with Beechcraft's new regime as Bleck cut back the Starship program and cancelled a number of promising programs including the Ares, Catbird, and Triumph. Bleck wanted to get rid of Scaled and agreed to let Burt acquire it at book value. "The main reason we wanted out of Beechcraft, was that Beech cancelled all our in-house general aviation research programs (cost cutting via canceling almost all Beech I R&D) and refused to allow us to do a general aviation program for a Beech competitor," Burt recalled. "Thus, I then reasoned that I was the only one in America that could not do general aviation research - my favorite thing to do!"

Burt had remained in touch with Walsh and knew of Walsh's continued interest in Scaled. In November 1988, Beech sold Scaled to a company formed by Burt called WUTTA (watch us this time around) and WUTTA sold Scaled to Wyman-Gordon, the company Walsh now headed. It was a good marriage. Although Walsh resigned from Wyman-Gordon in May 1991, Dave Gruber became president and maintained an excellent relationship with Burt and Scaled. Scaled remained a subsidiary of the company for the next twelve years. Under Gruber's tutelage, Scaled opened its Montrose, Colorado, facility and was able to expend funds on a number of unique and interesting projects for A-list customers including: Israeli Aircraft Industries, Loral, Lockheed, Orbital Sciences Corporation, Northrop, Sandia National Laboratories, Bell Helicopter, McDonnell Douglas, the Department of Energy, Zond, NASA, and Space Industries.

Many of Scaled projects were enveloped in secrecy. However, some of the secret work was not related to military or government projects. For example, Toyota contracted Scaled to develop an aircraft designed for the Japanese giant and employing an aviation liquid-cooled version of the Lexus LS400 engine, a project that has been shrouded in mystery and secrecy from inception. In 2002, journalist Peter Pae of the *Los Angeles Times* wrote, "After initially refusing to talk about the program, a spokesman confirmed that forty aerospace engineers, hired away from some of major aerospace concerns such as Boeing Co. and Raytheon Co., have been working on the aircraft for at least four years."

The New York Times in 1995 described some of the more esoteric projects with which Burt was involved: "the Raptor, a high-altitude unmanned aircraft commissioned as a missile-killer by the Strategic Defense Initiative . . . , wings for the Pegasus, a privately built rocket that is launched from a converted L-1011 airliner, and the aeroshell (or fuselage) of the McDonnell Douglas DC-X, a re-usable, Buck Rogers-like rocket that has demonstrated the ability to blast off conventionally and then, balanced on its exhaust plume, descend to its launching pad."

The broad scope of Burt's reputation in design can be measured, in part, by a variety of non-aviation-related projects presented to him. To defend the 1988 America's Cup races, the San Diego Yacht Club and Dennis Conner syndicate decided to build two catamarans, one with a soft sail, the other with a revolutionary rigid sail designed by Scaled. Burt's boat, the rigid-sale version of *Stars & Stripes*, proved to be faster and Dennis Conner used her to successfully defend the cup. Burt also constructed the Ultralight, a one-hundred-mile-per-gallon, four-passenger automobile show car for General Motors in 1991. Which brings up Burt's history as a practicing, non-pedantic, non-activist environmentalist.

THE PYRAMID

The Mojave Desert is one of the hotter places in North America with temperatures well above one-hundred degrees in the summer. But in the winter, temperatures can dip into the teens and snowfall is not unknown. This broad range in temperatures makes living there a challenge. Air conditioners are ubiquitous in all homes as are heaters for the cold nights and colder winters. These HVAC units consume considerable energy and money. Burt, who could not pass up an opportunity to find a simple solution to a problem decided to tackle the desert's unforgiving climate while building his home in Mojave.

"I planned a super-insulated structure … so the house would have provisions for a semi-active, semi-passive solar heating and cooling system," he told *Popular Science*. Although his plans called for a square structure, working with the architect, the house turned into a six-sided pyramid, a thirty-one-hundred square foot house with a hexagonal garage and a south-facing entrance. Bermed on the outside, leaving only the top of the pyramid exposed, the house used about 15 percent of the energy of a typical house in Mojave. According to *Popular Science* in 1989, in a lengthy article entitled *21ˢᵗ Century Pyramid: the Ultimate Energy-Efficient House*: "The pyramidal roof would capture rising interior heat that could be recirculated during the winter, vented in the summer." A collection of ponds and a water wheel combined with stone and rocks made the house super efficient, requiring little cooling or heating. "There's lots of thermal mass among the rocks and ponds," Burt said. "It gets cold enough to snow here in the winter, but a couple of logs in the wood stove is all I need to heat the house. And long after the fire goes out, there will

Figure 26 Burt Rutan's Pyramid House in Mojave, California, with his GM EV1. Courtesy of Burt Rutan.

be warmth coming out of the rocks and water that I can move around the house."

The roof bore a familiar Rutan refrain—composites. *Popular Science* described it: "From the inside out it's plaster, then 12 inches of fiberglass insulation, then plywood, and a commercial rubber-plastic material for waterproofing. On top of that is a two-inch layer of Styrofoam, then tar paper, wire and several coats of stucco." The top was painted white to reflect light and heat.

The pyramid house is not the sole evidence of Burt's eco-consciousness. His principal car for seven years was the General Motors EV1, the first all-electric car mass produced in the United States. GM made only 900 EV1s which were leased, not sold, and Burt was one of the fortunate few to have it until General Motors ended the program and retrieved all the EV1s. And if this is not sufficient proof of Burt's ecologically-sensitive inclination, he built a solar water-heating system for RAF in 1978, one of the first commercial enterprises to employ such a system and long before it became fashionably green.

Boomerang, Proteus, and More

In late 1993 or early 1994, Burt started to design one of the most unusual, unique, and brilliant planes among his growing inventory of unconventional designs. It made a public splash at Oshkosh on August 1, 1996, landing in the middle of an air show. At first appearance it didn't look like a Rutan-inspired craft—the canard was missing. From a distance it even looked conventional, but as it approached the runway the Boomerang caused a series of double-takes as the spectators tried to understand what their eyes were telling them. It was a twin. Both engines were in front. Yet, everything else seemed awry. The fuselage was larger than the pod next to it. The twin vertical tails had a horizontal tail jutting out from the right vertical tail, but ended flush with the left tail. The wing looked like a boomerang, hence its name. The nose landing gear was to the left side of the main fuselage; the left main was on the pod or smaller fuselage. No one could understand how it could taxi in a straight line let alone fly in one.

But this was Burt's genius. He had developed a pressurized twin that would be relatively easy to fly with a single engine out, be nearly stall- and spin- free—"the boom can fly at full aft stick, single engine, with the pilot's feet off the rudder pedals, a very big safety advantage," Burt said. The numbers were most impressive: a range of more than twenty-three-hundred nautical miles at economy cruise, a climb rate of twenty-nine-hundred feet per minute at best rate of climb, five-hundred feet per minute on one engine, and fly at speeds over three-hundred miles per hours. In virtually every performance category it put to shame all twins of comparable size

Figure 27   The Boomerang. Courtesy of Burt Rutan.

and horsepower. To top it off, not as a pun on fuel, the craft was so efficient at economy cruise speeds it could get seventeen miles per gallon at more than two-hundred miles per hour. This would become Burt's personal plane.

Burt planned to unveil it to the public at Oshkosh after the Boomerang made its first flight on June 19, 1996. However, on its first flight a main gear collapsed on landing and the plane plowed into a ditch next to the runway at Mojave airport. No one was hurt, and the damage turned out to be superficial. On inspection, Burt discovered that there was no major structural damage to the fuselage due, in part, to the new composite material he employed in its construction. Also, though the propellers were unsalvageable, the engines were operational, and after working day and night to repair the damage, Burt, his wife Tonya, and son Jeff, flew the Boomerang non-stop to Oshkosh forty-two days later, covering the seventeen-hundred miles in just six-and-a-half hours at only 50 percent power. Still, its appearance belied its ability. *Popular Mechanics* said it "looks more like a trimotor that lost its right boom and engine." The Boomerang became Burt's favorite personal plane. "Anyone who flies multiengine general aviation will be shocked at the Boomerang's engine-out safety as well as performance," Burt said. "It's the most special, most significant general aviation airplane I've ever done."

The Boomerang also provided Burt an opportunity to work with his son, Jeff, who designed the data system for the craft. "It was the greatest adventure for me in our collaborative projects together," Jeff recalled. "I will never forget the thrill of the weeks I spent with my dad successfully integrating the system into the aircraft—followed by flying with my dad and Tonya to Oshkosh and arriving during the airshow.

Once committed to a project, Burt becomes completely immersed in it; this had not changed from the early years working on the VariViggen. For him, creativity and innovation are the fun part, but the work could also be stressful. The first of several health problems

Figure 28   The Boomerang, Burt's Favorite General Aviation Plane. Courtesy of Burt Rutan.

associated with his heart began in 1998 when he suffered a mild heart attack due to a blocked artery. His physicians performed an angioplasty to clear up the artery and placed a stent to keep it open. "After that I did not try to update my medical [pilots need periodic medical certificates to operate a plane] since I understood that it would involve a bunch more medical tests," he said. "I did not desire to ever fail an FAA Airman's medical." He continued to fly the Boomerang using a copilot serving as pilot in command. But his years of flying the Boomerang were sadly coming to an end.

Figure 29   The Proteus. Courtesy of Burt Rutan.

Development of another enduring and ultra sophisticated Scaled project, the Proteus, began around 1995 while Burt and Scaled were under the aegis of David Gruber at Wyman-Gordon. On September 23, 1998, Scaled announced the "unveiling of a new, special-purpose aircraft in a dramatic flight demonstration," witnessed by "Aerospace Officials from Industry and Government." This "inaugural event" demonstrated "the unique performance and flight characteristics" of a plane designed for flight at very high altitudes. Indeed, the flight characteristics of the Proteus were impressive. The twin turbofan was designed to fly above sixty thousand feet and remain on station for up to fourteen hours. It could be manned or unmanned.

Initially designed with telecommunications relays in mind, other potential missions were within its envelope of operations, including atmospheric research, commercial imaging, and most interestingly, "as a launching vehicle for space tourism." Even today its potential has expanded to approximately twenty different applications and continues to evolve. Accruing several flight records, including an altitude record of 63,244 feet in October 2000, the Proteus was listed as number six in *Time* magazine's one hundred best designs of 1998. *Time* said "Proteus has the body of an insect but the heart of a jumbo jet."

In May 2005, Northrup Grumman announced successful tests and demonstration of the ability to release a weapon—a five-hundred-pound inert weapon—from a medium-altitude, long-endurance unmanned aerial vehicle conducted over Nellis Air Force Base. It was the Proteus and Northrup confirmed that it anticipated its ability to "perform a variety of missions ranging from traditional intelligence gathering to weapons delivery." As recently as March 2011, Proteus was in the news as Northrup Grumman and NASA flew it in tandem with the Global Hawk to demonstrate the feasibility of aerial fueling by unmanned aerial vehicles.

In an attempt to revitalize general aviation and the light aircraft industry, in 1996 NASA entered into an agreement with Williams International, producer of airplane propulsions systems, to produce a smaller, lighter turbofan engine. Sam Williams, the company's chairman made a number of designs of a V-tailed four-seat jet, then entered into a contract with Burt to redesign and build the V-Jet II, a proof-of-concept turbofan-driven private jet that would replace piston-driven aircraft. It would showcase Williams new "FJX-2 high bypass ratio engine characteristics in flight over the anticipated speed and altitude range for the future 'turbofan-powered, light aircraft era.'" Williams declared, "Burt Rutan and his team have made major improvements to the design and have introduced into this prototype many new, exciting manufacturing processes." The jet, test-flown by Doug Shane, made an appearance at Oshkosh in July 1997, enthralling the crowds with its sleek, futuristic design. However, the craft never went into production. It is now at the EAA Museum in Oshkosh, looking as ultramodern today as it did nearly fifteen years ago.

But the halcyon days at Wyman-Gordon were ending. Precision Cast Products acquired Wyman-Gordon and Burt was once again faced with the unwelcome prospect of corporate succession and executives who were not thrilled with Scaled or failed to understand

PCP

Figure 30 Williams V-Jet II, redesigned and built by Scaled now resides at the EAA Museum in Oshkosh, Wisconsin. Courtesy of Burt Rutan.

its capability. Northrop, Scaled, and Wyman-Gordon's David Gruber could see the remarkable potential of the craft Scaled was producing and its prospects for a successful business, so the question arises why Precision Cast Products was so blind and terminally dumb about Scaled's value to their organization.

Immediately after the acquisition of Wyman-Gordon, Precision put Scaled up for sale. After undergoing abrupt executive shifts with three different CEOs and experiencing the negative consequences, Burt had had enough. He had firsthand knowledge of how easily his future could be manipulated and potential projects and business impeded if he didn't have control.

Burt had two principal concerns about a sale of Scaled by Precision. If Scaled was acquired by some company with whom he would not fit well, it would be, as Yogi Berra said, "déjà vu all over again," with the same set of problems he had faced with the Raytheon ownership. Secondly, one of the reasons for Scaled's success was its ability to get business from all aircraft companies and the military establishment. If they were acquired by a major aerospace firm, it would end Scaled's ability to bid or seal a deal on a variety of interesting projects. So Burt and ten investors, including Dave Gruber and Mike Melvill, formed Scaled Composites LLC in September 2000 and purchased the assets of the Scaled division of Precision Cast Products for six million dollars. When one of the investors withdrew, Burt purchased his share. So Burt anted up twice for Scaled and stayed on as CEO of the company.

Scaled Composites LLC had a promising future. The relationship with Northrop, another investor in Scaled, holding a 39 percent ownership interest, was blossoming. Scaled and Northrop had been working together on several projects including the privately-funded, futuristic-looking Pegasus, a proof-of-concept diamond-shaped, tail- and fin-less, unmanned combat vehicle, designated as the X-47A. The rollout ceremony took place in July 2001, and the first flight took place in February 2003. Like the Proteus, the newer iteration of the Pegasus, the X-47B, is currently in the news, undergoing

Figure 31   X-47A Rollout. Courtesy of Scaled Composites LLC.

aircraft carrier operations tests for the U.S. Navy. The positive experience and confidence Northrop Grumman gained from its day-to-day dealings with Scaled and recognizing Scaled's future potential, led it to acquire the remaining 61 percent of Scaled for approximately $61 million in cash in 2007. Essentially, Scaled Composites is now Northrup Grumman's Skunk Works. And as if to underscore this similarity to Lockheed's top-secret facility that developed two remarkable spy-planes, the U-2 and the SR-71 Blackbird, Scaled has developed a prototype of a new spy plane, the Firebird.

SECOND BLOCKBUSTER — SPACESHIPONE

Burt's fascination with space exploration can be traced to his childhood, watching Disneyland's "Man in Space," and later the X-15 rocketing into space, the Mercury, Gemini and Apollo capsules firing into orbit, and Neil Armstrong's first steps on the moon. The 1960s were heady days. "I always had the space bug" Burt acknowledged. Later, as his aircraft designs and development became more sophisticated, he realized that he, too, could design a space capsule and "launch it from an airplane that did a steep climb and a parachute recovery."

Author Dan Linehan, in his excellent book, *SpaceShipOne: An Illustrated History* quotes Burt: "I was going to build something to fly out of the atmosphere. I'm not saying the things that I originally laid out were easy. They weren't easy, but they weren't really innovative. They were pretty straight forward. It didn't require anything that was new or patentable or breakthrough in nature." Burt said he was determined to do it. "I was going to [build the craft] come hell or high water no matter where I got the money."

Burt began sketching his ideas in 1993. His initial plans centered on a rocket-powered capsule launched at high altitude that would return to Earth with a "feathered" descent; that is, it would have components sticking out of the blunt end of the capsule that would serve like the feathers of a shuttle cock in badminton, letting the capsule reenter the atmosphere, decelerate, and float down to Earth under a parachute. The craft would have to travel at supersonic

speed, something only major aerospace companies with government help had ever built. It was a daunting task, and perhaps that
was one of those instances that brings out the best in Burt, going
after what others deem inconceivable—he was literally shooting
for the stars.

And the stars and planets were aligning properly for Burt and
Scaled in the mid 1990s. Several seemingly unrelated events con-
verged, but in retrospect turned out to be interrelated. Proteus was
evolving into the craft Burt envisioned as the launch vehicle. It
would climb to twenty-seven thousand feet, point its nose in a forty
degree upward trajectory and release the rocket-powered capsule
that would power its way into suborbital space, one-hundred kilometers above the Earth. The capsule-shuttlecock system would reenter
Earth's atmosphere and deploy a parachute for landing on water, or
preferably in the air, getting snatched by a helicopter to avoid the
dangers of a water landing.

Burt had met one of Paul Allen's associates, Vern Raburn, who
arrived at Oshkosh in a Lockheed Constellation he had purchased
from John Travolta. At the time, Allen, who co-founded Microsoft
with Bill Gates and was one of the twenty-first century's greatest
tycoons, was buying up cable companies. Burt asked Raburn whether
Allen might be interested in helping Angel Technologies develop a
broadband capability with continuous air presence based on the Proteus. In September 1996, Allen and Raburn flew to Mohave Airport
to meet Burt, arriving in one of Allen's private Boeing 757s. When
Burt saw the massive plane, he wondered how Allen would alight
since the airport didn't have any gateway or ladder tall enough for
the huge jet. But the door opened, a special stairway descended and
Allen clambered down.

"My first couple of meetings with Paul were not about space
at all," Burt said. The early discussions revolved around the Proteus and getting broadband coverage over Los Angeles with Angel
Technologies. In the discussions Burt discovered Allen "was a
space nut," fascinated by space and science fiction from his earliest

years; "few people know, he even has a science fiction museum," Burt said.

According to Allen, at a meeting held in Allen's offices in Seattle two years later, Burt first "floated his plan for a manned rocket flight into suborbital space." In his memoir, *Paul Allen Idea Man*, Allen writes: "Burt wanted to demonstrate that you didn't need NASA level resources to create a commercial space tourism industry and bring ordinary people to the same black sky that once greeted Alan Shepard."

"I'm looking for a way to do a small version of the X-15," Burt told Allen. "I'm not ready yet to put my own money in it, so the last thing I would do is ask someone else to do it." For Burt placing one's own funds at risk on a project was the ultimate ethical litmus test. He told Allen several times that he was not ready.

Figure 32   Paul Allen and Burt Rutan. Courtesy of Burt Rutan.

Burt focused on creating a better feathering system. He wanted to glide down to a landing instead of relying on a deployed parachute, and he did not like the projections sticking out of a capsule. To glide he needed wings, but he also needed a system to create drag to achieve a feathered reentry. In 1999, Burt had an epiphany—instead of having projections sticking out of the capsule, he would design wings, a portion of which would rotate to create drag on reentry, and when the craft was back in the atmosphere and feathered to a slower speed, the wings would pivot back and be deployed for the glide. He tested different designs by throwing models from the tallest building in Mojave – the airport tower.

According to *Time* magazine, "The reception was muted. Rutan was widely respected in the experimental-plane-building industry . . . But the design for SpaceShipOne inspired near universal derision." If anything would inspire Burt, it would be derision. When anyone tells him what he is pursuing is "nonsense," he believes he must be doing the right thing and moving along the right path.

Burt and Allen's visions of what they sought to achieve were not identical. Burt was looking at the bigger picture, taking people to space. Allen had a narrower, more defined view—to get the first astronauts to space and back in a privately financed venture. A careful man with computer-like analytical ability, Allen felt Burt was the right man for the job for several reasons, chief among them, the nearly inexplicable feat: "none of his designs had crashed during testing," Allen wrote. Moreover, Burt had already demonstrated his penchant for creating innovative and unique craft, like Voyager, that had ventured where no human had ventured before—and succeeded. Finally, there was Burt's reputation for completing projects on time and on the money.

Once he had a workable solution, Burt told Allen he could do it. "I said a few sentences to him," Burt recalled. "If he talks, don't step on him. Listen." Allen responded quickly, "Let's do it." "That was all the begging and money searching I went through for Space-ShipOne." It was one thing to have a handshake, it was another to reduce their agreement to writing. Allen's lawyers, protecting their client, introduced a number of ponderous terms and conditions. One in particular was a sticking point and unacceptable to Burt: if Allen were to unilaterally withdraw at any time, Burt would not be allowed take his designs to anyone else or continue with the project. "I would have been the only one in America unable to do it," Burt said. Fortunately for posterity and history, Allen and Burt resolved the problem.

Allen's involvement as the financial backbone of the SpaceShipOne program remained a secret for years. Even as late as December 2003, the *New York Times* reported: "SpaceShipOne is backed by a company that is interested in space tourism. Mr. Rutan would not name this customer, though some reports say the backer is Paul Allen, the co-founder of Microsoft."

Burt was ready to enter into the agreement in his name, but in discussions with Scaled's board of directors and mindful that the deal with Allen would represent a legal corporate opportunity for Scaled, Burt substituted Scaled in his place. Scaled and Allen's company, Vulcan Ventures, formed Mojave Air Ventures LLC (MAV) after the contract was signed in March 2001. Burt estimated that the cost of developing a three-man spaceship (including the launch airplane, the rocket motor and all the testing) would be about eighteen million dollars. It was completely funded by Allen who retained a majority interest. The contract called for Scaled to build a simple launch craft, but subsequently Burt realized he should incorporate safety structures and space systems directly into the launch vehicle, the cost of which he had not contemplated when he produced cost estimates for Allen. Moreover, Burt had underestimated a number of other costs including program management, patents, marketing and promotion. Allen paid the bills, but reduced Scaled's equity in MAV accordingly. Allen expected MAV to generate income from licensing the technology Burt and Scaled would develop.

The formation of the X Prize Foundation by Dr. Peter Diamandis in 1995 was another event coinciding with the development of Proteus and the subsequent meetings between Burt and Allen. Diamandis proposed the X Prize to the NSS International Space Development Conference, to demonstrate a private vehicle capable of carrying a person to the edge of space. NASA was spending hundreds of millions of dollars for each Space Shuttle launch, and Diamandis wanted to encourage private companies to be creative and innovative, and achieve the goal of carrying passengers into space without government funding. Diamandis modeled the X Prize on the twenty-five thousand dollar prize Frenchman Raymond Orteig offered for the first person to fly solo across the Atlantic. Charles Lindbergh was one of several pilots who sought the lucrative prize. In total more than $400,000 was spent by various groups vying with Lindbergh, who won it in 1927.

When Burt learned about the X-Prize competition he secretly worked on design concepts. At the Foundation's gala event in St Louis in May 1996, Burt said that "if the prize got funded, he would go after it." News coverage of the Gala described Burt as the "front runner to win [it]," however, the SpaceShipOne program remained covert. "I never told Diamandis its schedule or that it was a MAV project. . . Peter did have a relatively good idea that we were probably working on a program, but we still had not registered an intent and a schedule with X-Prize organization. He knew without asking that we probably would not make it by the end of 2003." Burt's participation as a competitor was not officially revealed until the SpaceShipOne rollout in April 2003.

But like Dick Rutan and his quest for funding the Voyager project a decade earlier, Diamandis discovered that obtaining the ten million dollars necessary to fund the prize was more difficult to achieve than anticipated. He managed to raise five million dollars from various sources in St. Louis and other donors in May 1998 and announced it at the Smithsonian's Air & Space Museum next to *The Spirit of St. Louis*. But without complete funding, Burt and Allen could not count on it and Burt was skeptical about the X Prize Foundation's potential for success. Initially, "Allen wasn't interested in the X Prize." Burt said. "It was more important to him that we wouldn't embarrass him with a failure."

In 2002, Anousheh and Amir Ansari agreed to become the title sponsors of the renamed Ansari X Prize, and purchased from Progressive Insurance Company a ten million dollar insurance policy known as a "Hole-in-One," a policy commonly found in golf tournaments where an insurance company bets that the odds of no player getting a hole-in-one are in its favor. The X-Prize insurance policy was to expire on December 31, 2003; however, Diamandis feared Burt would not go after the X-prize because it would be too late and arranged for the insurance policy to be extended through the end of 2004.

The X Prize terms and conditions were specific: the spacecraft had to take the equivalent of three people (a pilot and two dummies weighing a minimum of six hundred pounds) to an altitude of one hundred kilometers, return to Earth, and repeat the flight in the same craft within two weeks. Progressive Insurance Company was betting it would not happen. Twenty-six groups from seven different countries were soon competing with MAV for the prize. Once the X Prize was funded, Allen saw it as a means of recouping part of his investment.

Figure 33   White Knight above and Proteus below. Courtesy of Burt Rutan.

After the agreement between Scaled and Allen was executed in March 2001, and funding became available, Burt began the complex and arduous task of building the first civilian, non-governmental-funded space vehicle. Construction of the launch vehicle, named White Knight by Scaled employee Cory Bird, and the spacecraft, named SpaceShipOne by Burt, began in earnest. "Almost everybody hated both names," Burt admitted, "but no one could come up with anything better. . . I could call it whatever I wanted. .. Spaceships only existed in books like Buck Rogers . . . This is a spaceship. No one had called a manned spacecraft a 'Spaceship' before." The names stuck and subsequently when Sir Richard Branson became involved, he adopted the name for his Virgin Galactic venture, calling the commercial design types White Knight Two and SpaceShipTwo, but as with his airliners, he renamed White Knight Two *Eve* and Space-ShipTwo V.S.S. *Enterprise.*

Allen was impressed by Burt's small and exceptional team. "The remarkable thing about MAV," he wrote, "was that it built a manned space program from scratch . . . And they didn't just engineer a spacecraft, they also built the launch airplane, flight simulator, avionics system, and rocket motor test facility." Burt also built backup parts for SpaceShipOne because he told Paul Allen he would have a backup in case the first one crashed. But they never had to assemble a second spaceship.

In 2002, Burt was diagnosed with a ten percent or greater possibility of a "sudden-death heart attack" due to electrical faults of the heart. Physicians implanted a pacemaker/defibrillator and Burt was soon back at work. However, given his medical condition, he had to abandon one of his loves: flying his own craft, especially the Boomerang.

One area where much has been written, often inconsistently or inaccurately, relates to the development of the most critical component of the SpaceShipOne project—rocket propulsion. Scaled had designed other aircraft around propulsion systems knowing they could buy, lease or get engines consigned to them. However,

SpaceShipOne presented a new challenge. Although there were solid-fuel and liquid-fuel rocket engines available elsewhere, none of them fit Burt's requirements. He knew how dangerous and expensive it was to ameliorate the risks inherent in such engines. He also wanted to be able to go at different speeds, increasing speed at each test of the motor, but with a solid-rocket ignition there is no way to shut it off. "I needed a rocket motor with either a throttle, where we could slowly accelerate or where we could shut it off at any time," he said. The inability to shut off a solid-fueled rocket engine could hurl SpaceShipOne into unknown and unplanned Mach speeds. "The X-15 could throttle," Burt said, "but it was a very complex motor; there were so many places it could leak or rupture. The same applied to other liquid-fueled engines" that were complex and dangerous.

Burt opted for a hybrid rocket engine, which, as the name suggests, combines both a solid fuel and liquid oxidizer. It is simpler and safer than liquid- fueled rockets, and like all liquid units, has throttling or shut-off capability. It is also safer than solid-fuel rockets. The genesis for Burt's interest in the hybrid dates back to his college days at CalPoly. In 1963, several engineering students built a hybrid rocket motor for their senior project using Plexiglas as the solid fuel. They simply pumped oxygen into a Plexiglas tube, ignited the gas and had a controlled burn. They were able to run the rocket and shut it off multiple times. Even hobbyists were building small hybrids using nitrous oxide—laughing gas—as the oxidizer and common rubber for the fuel; some were even using inexpensive asphalt for fuel!

Burt opted for a hybrid rocket engine where nitrous-oxide gas would flow from a tank to a chamber filled with rubber. When ignited, the burning rubber would emit jets of high-speed gas and provide powerful thrust for the spacecraft. He also conceived of a new way to configure a hybrid rocket engine, employing a skirt-mounted nitrous tank where all the rocket motor components were cantilever-mounted to the tank, leaving only one place where it could leak and no other mounts or flex joints were needed. "No one else had done it," Burt said. "It was the simplest way to configure a hybrid rocket motor." He considers this skirt-mounted cantilevered engine to be one of his most successful accomplishments and it represents one of the patents MAV subsequently obtained.

After discussing plans for building the motor with a score or more companies, Burt decided to develop the main large components of the new hybrid motor himself (the large nitrous tank and the fuel combustion chamber with its integrated nozzle). He then solicited bids for the development of the igniter, injector, valve, and electronic motor controller from two companies: Environmental Aeroscience Corporation (eAc) and SpaceDev. He could have gone to a company like Rocketdyne, but it would have cost MAV more than $40 million, well beyond what Allen would have been willing to bear. Burt insisted that the two vendors demonstrate the safety and performance of their components with live fire tests on Scaled's motor at the Mojave ground test site.

The live fire tests would be a true competition; the components that performed best on the ground would be the ones that would fly on SpaceShipOne. Tests conducted by these companies elsewhere would be on their dime, not MAV's.

Ultimately, both companies received contracts to build components for SpaceShipOne (eAc's fill and dump systems on the tank front and SpaceDev's hot components on the tank aft). During the test program the President of SpaceDev drew Burt's ire when he announced on SpaceDev's web site that the SpaceShipOne rocket motor was a SpaceDev development and even put the SpaceDev logo on a rocket motor Burt had sent him. Burt was so incensed he sent the owner a letter threatening a lawsuit because it was not true and they were under an agreement to not disclose information about the rocket motor without Scaled's permission. This was Burt's design and a Scaled-constructed rocket motor. Burt had no problem with SpaceDev's performance, the problem was solely with SpaceDev's president. After the president died, the problems with SpaceDev evaporated. "eAc toed the line to a T," Burt recalled.

Pulling themselves up by their own bootstraps, several other people have claimed an exaggerated role in the development of the skirt-mounted cantilevered hybrid rocket motor. Burt scoffs at such claims. None of these people were the principal or even subordinate designers or provided the inspiration for the SpaceShipOne rocket motor—it was Burt's invention from inception to SpaceShipOne's flight to the edge of space.

Burt and Scaled unveiled SpaceShipOne and White Knight One to the public on Friday, April 18, 2003, before a large crowd including Astronaut Buzz Aldrin, space-tourist Dennis Tito, legendary NASA spacecraft designer Max Faget, and Cliff Robertson. BBC reported, "Experts are taking the initiative seriously, saying that Mr. Rutan's track record and new technology put him on course to win the so-called X-prize for the first non-government spaceflight." The *New York Times* was in accord: "Other teams are competing for the prize, offered by a St. Louis group called the X Prize Foundation, but none have offered a show like the one Mr. Rutan presented today."

It was a scene out of science fiction with White Knight One, resembling something Hollywood would dream up for a raptor-like alien craft from another galaxy making a demonstration flight. And SpaceShipOne appeared eerily similar to some of the craft seen in the old Flash Gordon television series. The genesis of both craft was fairly obvious to many in attendance. One reporter said, "They're Rutan-designed aircraft, and you can see their beautiful lineage."

NASA, or "the other space agency" as Burt called it, learned about SpaceShipOne the same time the public did. However, as a courtesy to the Federal Aviation Administration, Burt gave them advanced notice seeking to generate good relations with the governmental agency. He briefed the administrator and associate administrator for space flight several weeks before the unveiling in April.

Figure 34   White Knight with SpaceShipOne tethered in flight. Courtesy of Burt Rutan.

Eight months later and after seven test flights tethered to White Knight One or gliding without power, SpaceShipOne was ready for the first powered flight. It was December 17, the centennial anniversary of the Wright Brothers historic flight at Kitty Hawk. SpaceShipOne was about to undertake a similar audacious step into history and space lore. Burt was heading into unchartered territory. Author Dan Linehan said it best: "Flying above Mach 1 was not the same as flying below Mach 1. Flying outside the atmosphere was not the same as flying within the atmosphere. And flying with a rocket engine was not the same as flying without a rocket engine."

White Knight One with Pete Siebold at the controls and Cory Bird as flight engineer, lifted from Mojave Airport with SpaceShipOne secured to its belly and released the spaceship at an altitude of 47,900 feet. Brian Binnie, SpaceShipOne's pilot, steadied the craft and kicked the rocket motor into action. Pressed back by the enormous acceleration and pulling more than 3g's he flew from 0.55 Mach to Mach 1.2 in just fifteen seconds. That's equivalent to the acceleration of a Ferrari going from zero to sixty in less than two seconds. The g-force kick when the engine ignites presses the eyeballs back into their sockets. Two historic milestones were broken: it was the first craft to go supersonic that was not built by an aerospace prime company with government help; and it was the first manned craft to fly with a hybrid rocket motor.

Gliding back to Mojave Airport, Binnie encountered an unexpected problem with his landing configuration. SpaceShipOne touched down hard, the left main landing gear broke away from its mount, and the craft veered left into the dirt, leaving long grooves before skidding to a rest in the desert sand. Allen and Burt rushed to the stricken craft, concerned about Binnie's welfare, but he was okay. At a press conference, Burt explained what happened: "That wasn't Brian's fault. It was the fault of us not doing the proper thing, and that is putting a heater on the damper so that it didn't freeze up on him on the landing approach."

WINNING THE X PRIZE

The damage was not as severe as they first thought, and three months later SpaceShipOne was back in the air. Then, after three more test flights, the main event was about to take place, the one that would land SpaceShipOne next to the *Spirit of St. Louis* at the Smithsonian. It was June 21, 2004, and Burt was planning to make the first commercial space flight by exceeding an altitude of 100 kilometers. Again, having never done it before, it was a test flight. Normally aviation companies do not perform flight tests with the public in attendance, given the risks inherent in such flights. Murphy's law applies: whatever can go wrong, will go wrong. One crash with the public watching could scrub an entire program and greatly embarrass the principles. Although SpaceShipOne now had seven test flights under its wing, the riskiest flight would be the first powered flight out of the atmosphere.

Allen wanted to have the broadcast and print media and VIPs present. Burt felt it was historically so important and unprecedented that the flight should also be open to the general public. "I wanted to have kids there so they could later tell their grandkids that they saw the first commercial spaceship fly to space." There was little risk to the public; when SpaceShipOne returned for a landing it was simply a glider; it would not produce any toxic gases from the rocket motor. The announcement of the impending flight brought about thirty thousand people to Mojave Airport. A local developer rented sixty busses from Los Angeles and bussed kids from two Lancaster schools to watch. Allen was there, so was Sir Richard Branson.

About two hours from launch, Burt noticed that he had some free time and he went over alone to the parking lot to help direct traffic, probably astounding those drivers and passengers who recognized him.

At 6:47 a.m., White Knight took off under a cloudless blue sky and spiraled slowly upwards to forty-seven thousand feet before releasing SpaceShipOne. Pilot Mike Melvill ignited the motor and in less than ten seconds was heading supersonic—not straight and level, but climbing steeply toward outer space. At sixty-thousand feet a sudden wind shear made SpaceShipOne yaw, then roll. Climbing at transonic speeds, SpaceShipOne's stick and rudder were becoming ineffective. Allen, sitting at Mission Control, recalls: "I jumped off my chair" expecting Melvill to abort. Melvill did not; it was not in his character to do so. For Allen, "All thoughts of the X Prize vanished." Melvill wrestled with the controls and finally corrected the problem, but in doing so he went off the planned trajectory and lost precious seconds of climb attitude. Melvill let the motor continue to run until it automatically shut down. When SpaceShipOne coasted to its apogee, Melvill was in weightless space. He took some M&Ms out and let them float in the cockpit where he knew they would be seen in the cockpit video.

The question on everyone's mind was whether SpaceShipOne had achieved the one-hundred kilometer (328,084 feet) milestone. The official result was 328,491 feet; they cleared it by a mere 407 feet. After the landing, SpaceShipOne was towed before the cheering crowds with Melvill standing on top of the craft, waving to thousands of admirers.

Burt spied a sign in the middle of the crowd: "SpaceShipOne Government Zero" alluding to the failure of the U.S. to launch any space vehicle for more than a year after the Columbia Shuttle disaster. Burt waded through the undulating masses and got the sign so Mike could show it to the world as he stood atop SpaceShipOne. By the end of 2004 a new sign could have read, "Rutan Three, Government Zero," or even "Rutan Three, Russia Two, U.S. Zero."

As a result of this achievement, the Federal Aviation Agency awarded Melvill his stripes as the first ever civilian astronaut pilot, and the Smithsonian asked Allen and Burt to donate SpaceShipOne to their Air and Space Museum. But this historic accomplishment had nothing to do with the X Prize. SpaceShipOne only carried Melvill; the X Prize required the equivalent of three people carried into space, though properly weighed and certified dummies could be substituted for live passengers. This amounted to a payload of six hundred pounds and questions remained whether the rocket motor was powerful enough to reach the edge of space with the heavier load. They would have to strip every unnecessary ounce from SpaceShipOne and provide more power to the rocket engine. Moreover, two flights would have to be completed within two weeks.

Three months later, on Wednesday, September 29, 2004, Rutan was ready for the first X Prize flight, dubbed X1 by the X Prize Foundation. On a cloudless morning over the Mojave desert, White Knight lifted off at 7:12 a.m. before a massive crowd of spectators. It took nearly an hour to reach 46,500 feet before it could release SpaceShipOne with Melvill at the controls. The motor ignited, Melvill pulled the stick back and the small spacecraft headed absolutely vertically toward its destiny with space. It was "a white-knuckle ascent in which the rocket ship began an unexpected series of rolls as it roared toward the top of its arc," the *New York Times* reported. It looked like a top spinning upward out of control and leaving a corkscrew-like contrail behind it. A pall of silence fell upon the stunned spectators.

SpaceShipOne went through twenty-nine rolls before Melvill could right the ship. Some on the ground were wondering whether Melvill was doing it intentionally. He was not. Uncertain whether he was reaching the necessary height, and despite the rolls and advice from Mission Control to shut off the engine, Melvill allowed it to burn even longer than originally planned before shutting it off. Executing the feathering reentry protocol to perfection, returning through the atmosphere and gliding towards the airport, SpaceShipOne suddenly did another roll—this time it was intentional—it was Melvill's victory roll. Melvill had taken SpaceShipOne to a height of 337,000 feet, clearing the one-hundred kilometer hurdle by a comfortable margin. When asked about his experience on this flight, Melvill said: "I just loved every second of it. Maybe I'm crazy. . . The rocket flew like a dream." The Foundation confirmed SpaceShipOne successfully completed the first leg of the X Prize.

At a briefing, Burt told reporters he had sent several items aloft on the flight including the slide rule he used at CalPoly and, most importantly, his mother Irene's ashes. "She flew today," he said, his voice cracking.

The unexpected rolls forced the MAV-Scaled team back to the drawing board to analyze the problem. By nightfall they had determined what happened and, working in the simulator, learned what they needed to do to avoid a repetition of it. They had only two weeks to get the next flight up successfully. Burt planned for the possibility of making two more flights in that time period in case one of the flights did not reach the required altitude; he had three rocket motors available. Scaled resolved the problem quickly. "We could have gone up again by the weekend," Burt said, but he decided to wait until Monday, October 4, to send SpaceShipOne after the X Prize. It would leave him enough time to try again within the two-week deadline for the X Prize if this flight failed.

The journey began before 7:00 a.m., as White Knight lofted SpaceShipOne to the drop-off altitude of 47,100 feet. For pilot Brian Binnie, sitting in the lonely cockpit of SpaceShipOne, the hour-long ride to the release point must have seemed like an eternity with little to do but contemplate the magnitude of what he was about to do. Upon release, Binnie ignited the motor, then followed a trajectory designed to prevent the roll Melvill had experienced in the first X Prize flight. Pulling the stick back to a sixty degree ascent, and slowly egging the ship up to an eighty-eight degree climb, Binnie let the engine run for ninety seconds. It was dramatic, and SpaceShipOne not only reached the one-hundred-kilometer objective, it surpassed it by nearly seven and a half miles. Three milestones were achieved simultaneously: winning the X Prize, breaking the X-15 altitude record by thirteen thousand feet, and becoming the first craft, including government-sponsored and funded ones, in the history of space travel to go to space and return twice within five days.

Writing in his memoir, Allen recalled that daunting twenty-four-minute flight as Richard Branson, sitting next to him at Mission Control muttered "Paul, isn't this better than the best sex you ever had?" Allen didn't respond, but what he thought was apropos: "If I was this anxious during any kind of interpersonal activity, I couldn't enjoy it very much."

The landing before tens of thousands of spectators was a reflection of the entire flight—it was perfect and incident-free. A pickup truck

Figure 35 Paul Allen, Burt and Sir Richard Branson sitting on tailgate as SpaceShipOne is towed in front of large crowd after successfully completing the second flight to win the X Prize. Courtesy of Burt Rutan.

with Burt, Allen, and Branson sitting on the tailgate, towed Space-ShipOne before the thousands of cheering spectators, many shouting "Burt! Burt!," with Binnie standing atop waving the American flag he brought with him on the flight. And Allen, a very private and reserved person did something completely out of character; he suddenly made his way to the crowd, shaking hands and signing autographs, completely immersed in the remarkable moment. Burt thought this was wonderful. Later, celebrating the success of the mission with champagne, Burt and Allen received a phone call from President George Bush calling them "true American heroes" congratulating them "for opening up the space frontier" and showing their "spirit of entrepreneurship."

Figure 36   (left to right) Doug Shane, Mike Melville, Burt Rutan, Paul Allen and Brian Binnie with the Robert J. Collier Trophy. Courtesy of Burt Rutan.

Col. Rick Searfoss, a former astronaut and the head of the panel of judges that certified the results, announced, ''I declare that Mojave Aerospace Ventures has indeed earned the Ansari X Prize.''

Time magazine put Burt and SpaceShipOne on its cover and joined in the accolades: "For solving the problems of suborbital flight and re-entry with ingenious design, for boldly going where NASA now fears to tread and returning without a scratch, but most of all for reigniting the moon-shot-era dream of zero-gravity for everyone, SpaceShipOne is TIME's Coolest Invention of 2004."

The National Aeronautics Administration (NAA) awards the Robert J. Collier Trophy annually for the greatest achievement in aeronautics or astronautics in America based on actual use in the preceding year. According to NAA: "The list of Collier winners represents a timeline of aviation, as many of the awardees mark major events in the history of flight." The list includes such aviation luminaries as Orville Wright, Glenn Curtis, Howard Hughes, Charles Yeager, Clarence L. "Kelly" Johnson, and Neil Armstrong. Burt had already received one Collier trophy; he was an award-winner in 1986 as designer of Voyager, joining only Curtis and Johnson as a recipient of two of these prestigious awards. When contacted about being nominated for the 2004 award, Burt told NAA that Paul Allen was equally deserving of the award. "A funding source doesn't get a Collier," Burt said, but Allen deserved this because of his "vision and the courage to take his own money and fund this. . . [but he] was not just a bank; without what he did and the courage to risk his reputation if it failed—he still did it—the things he did in the three years were critical to the success of the program." NAA agreed with Burt and awarded the Collier to Burt, Allen, Doug Shane, Melvill and Binnie. Burt is also the only recipient of two Doolittle trophies (awarded by the Society of Experimental Pilots for engineering or management accomplishment).

Half of the $10 million X Prize went to Scaled. Burt took this money and allocated it to all Scaled owners and employees from the executives to the floor sweepers, reflecting his pride and appreciation in what they had done. For Burt the success of SpaceShipOne program

Figure 37 Sir Richard Branson and Burt. Courtesy of Burt Rutan.

was a collective and collaborative effort and he treated it accordingly. He was particularly proud that the cost overrun on the original 2000 estimate given to Allen for the enumerated tasks was only about ten percent. Allen noted in *Idea Man*: "Based on what I'd heard about bleeding-edge aircraft, I expected SpaceShipOne to come in overweight, underpowered, over budget, and behind schedule."

The feat was precedent setting in many ways. On October 4, 2004, the *New York Times* reported: "The successful completion of the X

Prize competition could usher in a new age of commercial human space flight. Several companies are already in the running to bring tourists to space. Sir Richard Branson announced a new company last week, Virgin Galactic, to commercialize Mr. Rutan's technology." At dinner on June 20, 2004, the night before Melvill's historic flight to the edge of space, Burt, Allen, and Branson discussed the possibility of working together on the development of private space travel. "I left the evening feeling uplifted," Branson said. "I had always felt that the government monopoly on space was a danger to mankind rather than the benefit often touted by cynical politicians and self-serving missile manufacturers."

Initially, Burt wanted to continue to work with Allen on a commercial version of SpaceShipOne, but after the Smithsonian asked for SpaceShipOne, Allen declined to get into the commercial side of the business. In a manner of speaking he had reached his apogee with SpaceShipOne.

SpaceShipOne began its final voyage from its home in Mojave to the Smithsonian's Air and Space Museum in Washington, D.C., on July 25, 2005. Since she would never fly again, Burt wanted to stop at the Oshkosh EAA airshow, his home away from home for the previous thirty years, and give his public a last view of the WhiteKnightOne and SpaceShipOne in flight, tethered together—a spectacular display with a landing in front of hundreds of thousands of people. WhiteKnightOne, piloted by Melvill first stopped at Madison, Wisconsin, to refuel. Burt met the crew in Madison, arriving in Robert Scherer's Starship along with Tonya and Mike's wife Sally. Burt was planning to board SpaceShipOne for the short flight to Oshkosh.

It was all planned with military precision, but what happened next was strictly an aberration from Burt and Scaled's normal practice of following strict protocols. Burt turned to Tonya and said, "No one has ever ridden in the back seat of SpaceShipOne before . . .Why don't you hop in and strap up."

Tonya was stunned. "It was an on-the-spot decision, completely unexpected," she said. "I heard a murmur behind me. The crew was all for it, all right, but I knew it was a rule-bender. 'The Ranger's not going to like that, Yogi,' I whispered to Burt. He thought for a moment, and in his best Yogi voice, answered philosophically, 'Wull. . . . @#!% the Ranger, Boo-Boo.'"

Tonya was mesmerized by the flight. "SS1's controls jiggled — a captive butterfly struggling to fly — we could feel the wind flow buffeting its wings," she said. "I felt good then. You could just tell, in the seat of your pants, that once SpaceShipOne was released it would fly, and it would fly well. Once released it would stop bucking, stop resisting its tight hold. You could feel its strength, even under the grip of the much stronger WhiteKnight. . . . It was electric . . . the most thrilling ride I've ever experienced." It was the only time in SpaceShipOne's history that it had two passengers aboard, three if one counts Burt and Tonya's "Tiger" the stuffed animal they traditionally carry on flights to Oshkosh.

Figure 38 Burt and Tonya Rutan in SpaceShipOne on flight from Madison, WI to Oshkosh. Courtesy of Burt Rutan.

GLOBALFLYER

As if the White Knight and SpaceShipOne programs for MAV were not exciting enough as record breaking undertakings, Burt's Scaled Composites was simultaneously designing and building another unusual craft for adventurer Steve Fossett. Fossett sought to break several records: the solo, non-stop flight around the globe and the distance record for a non-stop flight set nearly two decades earlier by another Burt-designed craft—Voyager.

Burt created the preliminary design for the GlobalFlyer (the detail design was done by Jon Karkow), a single-jet-powered aircraft made of composite material that weighed only thirty-three hundred pounds, but had a 114-foot wingspan, the length of a Boeing 737-700's wings. With tanks designed to hold twenty-five thousand pounds of fuel, GlobalFlyer was a record in itself—no plane in history had ever had such a high ratio of fuel to empty weight, not even Voyager. The GlobalFlyer made its maiden flight in March 2004, just three months before Melvill's record-setting flight in SpaceShipOne. It would not be an understatement to say Burt's plate was full in 2004 and 2005, as one Rutan-designed craft after another performed record breaking feats in aviation and space. Fossett succeeded in piloting GlobalFlyer to major records including the first solo non-stop flight around the world, accomplished between February 28 and March 3, 2005, and nearly a year later breaking the absolute distance-without-landing record set by aircraft—Voyager—or by Bertrand Piccard and Brian Jones in a balloon.

Writing in *Time* magazine in 2005, astronaut James Lovell, who flew on the first manned-mission to orbit the moon, said:

"[Y]ou can't buy brilliance like Rutan's. . . he designed the Voyager aircraft that made the first nonstop flight around the world in 1986 and the GlobalFlyer aircraft that recently made the first such flight with a solo pilot. But it was SpaceShipOne that truly soared."

Figure 39 Steve Fossett's GlobalFlyer. Courtesy of Burt Rutan.

VIRGIN GALACTIC AND THE SPACE SHIP COMPANY

In late September 2004, a deal had been struck between MAV and Branson's company Virgin Galactic to employ MAV's patents in the development of new craft, White Knight Two and a larger space vehicle, one capable of carrying two pilots and six passengers to an altitude of approximately eighty-five miles, thirty-five kilometers higher than SpaceShipOne.

On July 27, 2005, Scaled and Virgin Galactic issued a joint public release announcing the formation of The Space Ship Company: "Sir Richard Branson (Founder, Virgin Group of Companies) and Burt Rutan (President, Scaled Composites) announced their signing of an agreement to form a new aerospace production company to build a fleet of commercial sub-orbital spaceships and launch aircraft. The new company will own the designs of the new SpaceShipTwo (SS2) and WhiteKnighTwo (WK2) launch systems that are now in development at Scaled Composites. The SS2/WK2 system will use the 'Care-free reentry' and the 'cantilevered-hybrid' rocket motor technology developed for the Ansari X prize-winning SpaceShipOne (SS1)." However, subsequently the detail designers of the new large hybrid rocket motors made major changes to the rocket motor concept, and abandoned the patented cantilevered design.

"I am very excited to have agreed to the terms on which we can now move forward to develop the world's-first commercial, passenger-carrying Spaceships," Burt said. "This will truly herald an era of personal spaceflight first described by the visionary science fiction writers of the 1940s and 1950s. Richard and I share a vision that commercially viable and safe space tourism will provide the foundation for the human colonization of space. I am looking forward, (actually looking way up!) to working together with Richard on this next exciting phase."

The development of any new craft involves risk, and although Burt had a stellar record of no fatalities in forty-three years of developing new aircraft, nearly every one a proof-of-concept employing new technology, the good fortune came to a grinding halt on July 26, 2007. It was not a crash, but an explosion on the ground that took place during a nitrous fuel-flow test at Scaled for Branson's Virgin Galactic SpaceShipTwo. The blast, heard several miles away, killed three men and injured three others. The explosion did not involve a rocket firing, rather it was when the nitrous oxide was flowing through an injector while Scaled was testing new components. It was a tragic event in Burt's otherwise flawless and unprecedented career. Burt was devastated. The *London Times* reported, "Journalists on the scene said he appeared distraught, hugging the airport manager and fire chief, and his voice broke as he relayed what happened." His immediate concern was not for the project, but for the families of the dead employees and for the injured.

The accident drained Burt emotionally. He would wake up each night with a cold sweat at 2:00 or 3:00 a.m. "I started to feel sick and weak and had a very severe case of insomnia," he recalled. "The weakness continued to get worse for five months until I could hardly walk. On the first of February 2008, I checked into emergency at UCLA Medical center and finally, a week later, they figured out what might be my problem. Within twenty-four hours they opened me up, removed the hardened pericardium enveloping my heart, and I got well right away. Constrictive pericardium is rare and difficult to diagnose. The chief heart surgeon at UCLA told me the night before that he had never done the procedure [before], even though he does three or four bypasses per day." Burt concedes that his medical problems may have been related to the accident; and even when he talks about the accident now, one can see in his eyes the sadness he still feels for the lost men and their families.

The accident did not dampen Branson's enthusiasm for the project. "I'm grateful to Richard for sticking with us," Burt told John Johnson, Jr. of the *Los Angeles Times*.

According to Allen, "By early 2006 Virgin Galactic had $13 million in deposits for rides on the VSS *Enterprise* (SpaceShipTwo was renamed by Branson) at $200,000 per head." Actually, Branson did not rename SpaceShipTwo and paying passengers are not likely to fly on VSS *Enterprise*, but on the next iteration of SpaceShipTwo. The number went up to thirty million dollars in 2008 with more than two hundred firm reservations. If White Knight One and SpaceShipOne were impressive science-fiction-like craft, the next generation of spaceships coming out of Scaled were even more spectral and futuristic, and considerably larger. White Knight Two wing span is nearly the equal of a Boeing 767. Although Branson was unduly optimistic about flying space passengers as early as 2007, between the nitrous-flow accident and the complexity of the project, VSS *Enterprise* did not complete its first glide flight until October 2010. Only recently, on May 4, 2011, in its seventh glide flight, did it complete its first successful "care-free" feathered reentry flight. More telling, it was the third glide flight in just twelve days. "I'm betting it will succeed," Allen said. Most experts agree.

Figure 40 Sir Richard Branson and Burt Rutan in front of WhiteKnighTwo and SpaceShipTwo. Courtesy Virgin Galactic.

BURT THE GOLFER

Burt is now an avid golfer, a sport he took up passionately after 1998 when his medical condition prevented him from keeping his pilot's license current. Unable to hop into the cockpit of his Defiant or Boomerang, Burt needed some other outlet to deal with the stress of work and settled on golf. "After I lost my medical to fly 12 years ago, I began working on my golf game," he told Kathy Strong of *Palm Springs Life*, while at his week-end home in PGA West at La Quinta, California. "In fact, I did find that it is just as rewarding to hit a green with a 3-wood as to make a good crosswind landing; maybe because the golf shot is a lot harder to do." Still, the inventor in him would not just settle for improving his game. "I created an 'Arctic hat' to wear for golfing in the heat. I also built a composite putter – not to market it, just for the fun of it."

Even after his heart surgery in 2008, Burt found other uses for golf. He played a round with NASA's Peter Smith. Joe Barmann, writing in the *Washington Post*, made the following calculation: "Rutan, space flight pioneer + Smith, nation's leading Mars authority + golf, male-bonding session = irresistible story." Burt participates in several major celebrity tournaments annually including the Bob Hope Classic, always dressed in vintage golf regalia. For example, after journalist Bargmann arranged for Burt to play at New Jersey's Baltusrol Golf Club, he was stunned by Burt's presence. "The imposing 6-foot-3 Rutan showed up at the notoriously fusty club outfitted in tartan-plaid plus fours, a matching tam

Figure 41 Burt wearing his ice-water-cooledarctic hat. Courtesy of Burt Rutan

o'shanter, a long-sleeved golf shirt, knee socks and suspenders. My first glimpse of him on the practice putting green will be with me forever."

Figure 42 Burt Rutan in his typical golfing attire. Courtesy of Burt Rutan.

BURT AND EXECUTIVE MANAGEMENT

As he recovered from heart surgery, Burt withdrew as Scaled's president in 2008. He had been in charge of RAF for thirty-five years and at Scaled for more twenty-six years, managing high-skilled engineers in the development of state-of-the-art aircraft, but he was not from the mold of typical CEOs. Doug Shane, who assumed the gavel as president of Scaled in 2008, first met Burt while a college student at the Flight Research Center of the University of Kansas. He visited the Rutan Air Factory in 1980 and found Burt to be a "very charismatic, focused, excited, and enthusiastic engineer who was very approachable." Then on winter break of his senior year, Shane took a "shot-in-the-dark" and called Burt to see if he had any job openings. It was 1982, and Burt told him he was forming a new company, Scaled Composites.

Shane went to work for Scaled in May and has been there ever since, so with twenty-eight years of working for and with Burt he has had an excellent window into Burt's management style. Burt was "very motivating, and very motivated," Shane said. "He led by example. He was the hardest working guy in the group, so everybody tried to keep up with him. . .we worked a lot of hours but he made it fun. He never felt like a boss, but it was clear he was in charge. It was not management by consensus; he had a very clear idea of what he wanted and he made it clear to everybody."

Even when Shane joined the management committee, the working relationship with Burt did not change. Burt had a very straightforward management philosophy, Shane said. "He always believed it wasn't about the money; it was about doing a good job. So he was motivated . . . and wanted to make sure we were all doing the fun stuff—things that were technically challenging or had never been done before." He never seemed to "worry about sales or growing the company." Burt built an environment where people enjoyed their work. He made it challenging and his employees responded with a generous dose of productivity.

The Bipod – Not Last And Not Least

Burt retired from Scaled on April 1, 2011. But the four months before his retirement were filled with the fun of developing another unique Rutan product, the Bipod. Burt wanted to go back to his roots: to work hands-on in the shop, getting greasy and dirty, rubbing hands with engineers, fabricators and other shop workers on something that intrigued him, something new and unlike anything he had done before.

On July 15, 2011, *Aviation Week* described the Bipod as "a two-seat, hybrid-electric roadable aircraft." Consisting of two pods connected by a horizontal spar between the pods, it can be driven like a car, or flown like an airplane. It was "originally conceived as a rapid, low-cost electric testbed, the effort evolved into a flying car and was accelerated to allow Rutan, a long-time advocate of personal electric aircraft, to see the vehicle completed before his retirement." It took just four months for the Bipod to go from preliminary design to its first flight. It has gone through several iterations, but the latest has two electric four-bladed propellers on the rear horizontal stabilizer. The Bipod is designed to fly up to 760 miles at 100 mph, though it has a predicted top speed of 170 mph, and a range of 820 miles on a tank of gas for freeway driving – and 35 miles on just batteries.

An interesting facet of the BiPod is the location of the road-driving controls (a steering wheel and a brake pedal) in the left pod, while the flying controls (stick and rudder pedals) are in the right pod. Like the martial art of judo, Burt has always sought maximum efficiency

Figure 43 The Bipod, Burt's last design and development at Scaled Composites before retiring. Courtesy of Burt Rutan.

with minimum effort and the results would have earned him a 10th degree black belt [the highest belt] in aviation. Commenting on one of the benefits of the BiPod (which has separate cockpits connected by an open passageway in the wing), Burt's daughter, Dawn, noted, "Bipod is the perfect car for dating your daughter ... the boys can hold her hand, but nothing else! 'Here young man, take MY car!'"

BURT AND RETIREMENT

Today, touring the speaking circuit, where he has appeared for companies such as IBM, General Mills, UBS, Lenovo, Frito Lay, and Guidant Corporation or as a commencement or keynote speaker at his alma mater, CalPoly, the University of North Carolina, Berkeley's Haas School of Business, the University of Illinois, and many other organizations, Burt explains how to manage innovators and the differences in the tasks required of creative versus productive talent.

Burt is an extremely ethical man as a result of his upbringing and nature; it is as much a part of his constitution as his creative nature. "He was always motivated by doing the right thing technically and professionally," Shane said. A small incident in Burt's childhood reflects his sense of ethics and honor. When Pop attended USC and the family was eking out an existence in East Los Angeles, Burt, then a small child, took a candy bar from a store and did not pay for it. It gnawed on him enough as an adult, to prompt him to go back to the store fifty years later and give the owner—not the same owner—a $20 bill, explaining it was repayment for a theft from years gone by. One can only imagine the stunned expression on the man's face as the tall, confident stranger forced him to take the money. Burt left the store relieved of his childhood onus.

In April 2011, Burt formally retired from Scaled and moved into a beautiful home, one he calls his "Idahome Cabin," overlooking the lake on the outskirts of Coeur d'Alene, Idaho. Surrounded by thick evergreen forests of fir and pine and snow-capped mountains with ample rain and snow, the environment is far different and

The Management of Innovators

Manager's **only** tasks: Set goal and get funding.

- Set difficult goal (50% should say impossible).
- Reward achievement of goal (power of a prize).
- Let the innovator decide what risks to take.
- Leave them alone and keep others out.
- Applaud courage and expect multiple failures.
- Allow *fun.*

How to Achieve Breakthroughs
Creativity vs. productivity elements

• Productivity	• Creativity
– Managed by: Spec/Schedule	– Managed only by: Goal
– Involves: Analysis/Iteration	– Involves: invention/thought
– Process must be defined	– Process cannot be defined
– Accuracy is critical	– Accuracy unimportant
– Mistakes are bad	– Multiple failures expected
– Many can be trained to design	– Unclear who can create
– Can grade progress	– Can only grade goal (y/n)
– Sensible approach is desired	– Confidence in Nonsense is ok|

considerably farther from the arid and desiccated Mojave Desert than the physical distance suggests.

Interestingly, two of his unique aircraft came out of retirement a short time after Burt moved to Idaho. The Catbird, a pressurized single-engine plane with coast-to-coast range, and the Boomerang, a plane Melvill described as making "any general aviation, multiengine airplane look like a piece of garbage." The Cat had been hanging from the ceiling at Scaled while the Boomerang had been mothballed for years. At one time Burt considered donating the Boomerang to a museum, but could not find it in himself to do so. "We got it out and washed it, and I flat out could not bring myself to bring it down because it is the only example of this type in the world ... It just seemed criminal not to have it out there flying." Both craft made their appearance at the EAA AirVenture show at Oshkosh in July. Moreover, the Cat made a visit to its creator's home in Idaho in August, followed by the Boomerang a few weeks later.

The Rutan family is a close-knit clan. Burt is not only close to Jeff and Dawn, he has an enduring relationships with his stepdaughters, Jetta Zellner and Kye Quesinberry. As head of the clan Burt revels in the continuing close relationships he has established between all four children and their families. In 2008 ten-year-old Cole, Jetta's son, designed and built a LEGO version of SpaceShipTwo with Jeff's help. Since then, Cole and Jeff have built an entire fleet of RAF and Scaled craft out of LEGOs and displayed it at the EAA Museum at AirVenture 2011 in Oshkosh. Jeff's objective is to publish a series of activity books containing plans to build many of these RAF and Scaled LEGO models. Seems that history is about to repeat itself as Jeff embarks on a path similar to his father's—selling plans for building planes—among many other ventures.

Burt is not without controversy. In many ways he's the ultimate misanthrope and non-conformist who says what he thinks and in what he believes without regard to political correctness or its incompatibility with more popular views. More than one storm front has crossed his path, and the criticism at times can be scathing, especially when he presents his views on global warming, the pyramids of Egypt and alien life in the universe.

Keep in mind, Burt has probably been one of the most environmentally conscious and sensitive players on the globe. He puts his

Figure 44 (left to right) Cole, Burt and Jeff with a LEGO model of SpaceShipTwo presented to Burt for Christmas. Courtesy of Jeff Rutan.

money where his mouth is, building what *Popular Science* magazine called the "ultimate energy-efficient house." He installed a solar-water heating system at RAF in the 1970s before it became fashionable to jump on the environmental bandwagon. He is building a thirty-four-acre photo-voltaic solar energy farm, and his primary car for seven years was a zero-emissions EV1 beginning in1997. All the aircraft he designed were stingy when it came to fuel—he won the 2000 Lindbergh Award "because of his creative aircraft designs that reduce pollution and improve mileage." Even his latest creation, the Bipod, was designed to go 820 miles on a tank of gas. The point is that he's an active environmentalist, not an environmental activist.

So what does Rutan say about global warming and CO2? His views are set out in detail in "An Engineer's Critique of Global Warming Science," last updated in 2011, and available on the internet (http://rps3.com/Files/AGW/EngrCritique.AGW-Science.v4.3.pdf). He believes an engineering analysis is vastly different from that of scientists, and his views are from an engineering perspective. Essentially, Burt concludes that "the current rise of CO_2 in the atmosphere by human emissions has very little to do with planet warming. Natural (non-human activity effects) grossly overwhelm the human contribution to warming." Moreover, "Adding CO_2 to the atmosphere is beneficial for all plant life, increasing crop yields and increasing our 'green earth.'" He has a very negative opinion of the doomsday portrayers: "The Alarmist chooses to huddle inside his echo chamber, attacking messengers who arrive, but spends no time to carefully inspect the data that forms his opinion; nor to notice the reporting of fraud."

As for the green movement's effect on the evolution of clean-energy airliners, he's adamant: "Write this down," he told me, "seal it in an envelope to be opened in twenty years: 'airliners today still use the lowest cost energy sources available to them and that is either 1) the same fuels used in 2011, or 2) the result of a new breakthrough that was not known in 2011. If a breakthrough occurred from 2011 to 2031, it was developed because it featured a lower cost solution, not because it substituted a higher cost solution that lowered the release of CO_2 into the atmosphere.'"

Burt's views on the Egyptian pyramids are often misrepresented or taken out of context. For an accurate account of his views, see: (See: http://www.burtrutan.com/burtrutan/downloads/ObservationsPyramidFabricationTech.pdf. Likewise, his views on alien life and UFOs can be found at http://www.burtrutan.com/burtrutan/downloads/RutanIntroToJohnAxexanderUFOBook.pdf

Burt's views on these topics are not strident. At the AirVenture airshow at Oshkosh in July 2011 a college-aged girl approached him and challenged his views on global warming. She was soon joined by two of her friends. I watched him patiently and quietly explain his position and the science behind it. It had the appearance of a teacher talking to a student. He was not confrontational, did not raise his voice or become sarcastic, and when he finished all three girls thanked him for explaining his ideas. Whether he changed their

Figure 45 Nothing is wasted; Burt's Mojave Pyramid with mailbox made of airplane tail. Courtesy of Burt Rutan.

minds is unknown, but it was clear they respected him and appreciated his effort to discuss the issue with them in a rational, almost professorial manner.

His views may be controversial and he has engaged in extended dialogue and debate with many whose views differ materially from his. However, there is a modicum of mutual respect best evidenced by a video former CNN anchor Miles O'Brien sent Burt for viewing at his retirement party. O'Brien, in a sleeveless shirt, framed by a beautiful verdant setting with lush tropical vegetation around him, wishes Burt well and signs off, "from Fairbanks, Alaska, I'm Miles O'Brien." The complete video is available at http://vimeo.com/21848422 Burt loved it.

There is no question that Burt is one of the greatest creators and innovators of the twentieth and twenty-first centuries. Part of his success lies in his strongly-held view that fear of failure is a major obstacle to success, especially creative success. "I like to try something that doesn't work, realizing that if it doesn't work I've learned something valuable. But if I try only things that are known to work, that's low risk, good for the bean counters. You're not going to fail, but you absolutely, positively, remove your opportunity of having any kind of a breakthrough. You cannot discover something new unless you try something that is likely to not work. The guys who are the creators, the inventors, who are successful in coming up with breakthroughs, have to have confidence in nonsense." Burt has proven to be supremely confident in pursuing nonsense, and the results reside in many museums and will be included in future history books.

"You know," Burt told Andy Meisler of the *New York Times* back in 1995, "many people look back and say, 'Gee, this is a really boring time, compared to the 60's, when we went so quickly to the moon from first orbit.' But I've got a theory that this is just a kind of

Figure 46   VSS Enterprise. Courtesy of Virgin Galactic.

gentle pause. There's going to be a renaissance, a super renaissance, in the next 15 years." Burt may no longer be as sanguine about the "gentle pause." On July 22, 2011, after the final American shuttle flight landed, former NASA administrator Mike Griffin told BBC News, "When you push aside all the puffery and high-flying political announcements, with the landing of Atlantis, the human spaceflight program of the US will come to an end for the indefinite future." Accordingly, if there will be a renaissance, it will be attributable to Burt, SpaceShipOne, Scaled and Virgin Galactic's *VSS Enterprise*, and Americans who have the courage to take the big risks associated with venturing into Space.

When I told a friend who owns an executive jet I was going to meet Burt Rutan, he said "that's like meeting the Wright brothers." This view of Rutan is not unique. Professor Ann Karagozian, head of the UCLA MAE Energy and Propulsion Research Lab called his accomplishments "monumental," and said his "achievements in putting together these known technologies into novel and robust systems can be compared, I suppose, to what the Wright brothers did." I concur.

Jeff Rutan sums up his dad's legacy. "He is a living example of what can be accomplished with passionate dedication to quality and innovation. His enthusiasm, creativity and prolific success have inspired entrepreneurs in all fields of endeavor. He will surely be remembered as one of the giants in aviation history."

He has designed or invented unique airplanes, spaceships, rocket motors, energy-efficient homes, cars, arctic hats, a car that converts into an airplane, 100 mpg-automobile, winged sail for the America Cup competition, sailplane, a perpetual motion water wheel—don't ask—and much more. It has been quite a revolution; but despite his retirement I believe the Burt Rutan story and revolution are far from over.

So, what is now in store for Burt? Rumor has it that he is now designing a new airplane. Seems that with forty-five designs built in forty-three years—at least those we know about—it would be a bit hard for him to stop abruptly. Burt has said that even though

Figure 47 Russian Ekranoplan known as the "Caspian Sea Monster," a 554-ton behemoth.

[See the "Caspian Sea Monster" in flight: http://www.youtube.com/ watch?v=WlEt0bCeTy8&feature=related]

he is now surrounded by lakes and rivers he has no desire to buy a boat, and might build one instead. Back in 1993, Burt was part of a DARPA research effort focused on studying the Russian wing-ships and seaplanes. The twelve-man group of American engineers and scientists made several trips to Russia to see if that technology made sense for future US defense platforms.

The Russians had been the leading advocates of the new technology, where plane/ship would use ground effect to skim a few meters above the water at speeds comparable to high-flying craft, but with greater fuel efficiency, while ferrying hundreds of troops, weapons, or passengers. Taking off or landing in water also gave these wing-ships the same flexibility Pan Am sought when it first introduced amphibian craft like the Sikorsky S-38 in 1928—in the absence of ground facilities and airports, the amphibians could land or takeoff anywhere with just minimal facilities. Expensive ground amenities

Figure 48   Russian "Lun" Ekranoplan wingship with six missle launchers.

[See the Lun in flight: http://www.youtube.com/watch?v=OeUe6aV ib08&feature=related]

were unnecessary. Over a thirty-year period the Russians had built a variety of craft known as "Ekranoplans" from small trainers to the "Caspian Monster," a 544-ton behemoth. Burt was able to see some of these craft, including the well-armed and sinister, shark-faced "Lun."

After those trips, Burt spoke often about a desire to develop a small wing-ship, one that could convert to a conventional seaplane. When asked, Burt just smiled and reminded me that almost all of his designs are never revealed until they are flying.—I guess we will have to just stay tuned.

And while we stay tuned, new announcements about Burt's exploits will continue to roll off the presses. On December 13, 2011, Paul Allen announced that he and Burt had reunited to develop the next generation of space travel using a "revolutionary approach to space transportation: an air-launch system to provide orbital access to space with greater safety, cost-effectiveness and flexibility."

In launching Stratolaunch Systems Corporation, a new venture, Allen explained his long-term view of the demand for effective and

Figure 49 Stratolaunch Systems new massive launch vehicle should be flying in 2016. Courtesy of Stratolaunch Systems Corporation. See http://www.youtube.com/watch?v=sh29Pm1Rrc0

efficient systems of taking people and cargo to space. "I have long dreamed about taking the next big step in private space flight after the success of SpaceShipOne – to offer a flexible, orbital space delivery system. We are at the dawn of radical change in the space launch industry. Stratolaunch Systems is pioneering an innovative solution that will revolutionize space travel."

The company will work with Scaled Composites to build the largest aircraft ever built or flown with a 380-foot wing span, six Boeing 747 engines, and weighing in at more than 1.2 million pounds. It will carry a multi-stage booster manufactured by Space X, the company founded by Elon Musk. A third company, Dynetics, will build the mating and integrations system between the giant plane and the Space X booster. "I did the preliminary designs for the mega-motherships at Scaled starting in 1991," Burt said. "Recently I turned it over to the young designers who will carry it into the build phase."

So is Burt an aerospace legend, a space pioneer, the final frontiersman, larger than life and an Einstein of aerodynamics? Does he deserve all the accolades he has received? The answer to both questions is indisputably yes. When Sir Richard Branson begins ferrying tourists to suborbital space and Paul Allen's Stratolaunch takes cargo and passengers into orbit, and beyond, the common link in both cases will be Burt Rutan.

Figure 50 Stratolaunch Systems Corporation launch vehicle. Courtesy Stratolaunch Systems Corporation

Figure 51 Aircraft developed by Rutan Air Factory (RAF). Courtesy of Burt Rutan.

Figure 52   Scaled Composites earlier aircraft. Courtesy of Burt Rutan.

Figure 53   More Scaled Composites aircraft. Courtesy of Burt Rutan.

Figure 54   More Scaled Composites craft and other innovations. Courtesy of Burt Rutan.

AFTERWORD

When I spent time with Burt at his home in Idaho after his retirement he hinted at a project he wanted to pursue. Overlooking the lake below his home, he said he wanted to build a utilitarian craft that could land anywhere, on land, water, or snow. And the lake offered him an excellent proving ground for water take offs and landings. I assumed that given Burt's penchant for perfection and design innovations, that the plane would also have long range, low fuel consumption, great stability, low stall configuration and decent cruising speeds.

Today, we know more about this development—it's called the SkiGull. *Flying* magazine described it "as a retirement chariot of sorts to carry Rutan and his wife, Tonya, who is also a pilot, around the world." The SkiGull incorporates retractable landing gear that easily converts from a seaplane, to a ski-plane to the ubiquitous land-based plane. According to Burt, these conversions can be made in a matter of seconds, 1.5 to be exact. Burt wanted the SkiGull to have "ocean crossing range," for example to go nonstop to Hawaii from the mainland without reserve tanks.

"Imagine going to snow fields anywhere there is around 400 feet of relatively smooth snow, or to a dirt patch right at Puma Punku," Burt said, "or any part of the Amazon, including the tiny rivers that feed it. Imagine doing an eight-month exploration trip around the world without ever going to an airport." What pilot in his right mind wouldn't want to have a plane like that?

The SkiGull is aptly named because looking up at the plane from the ground, its wings resemble a gull gliding through the air. Flight testing began in November 2015, but Burt explained that the SkiGull has a ways to go before he would be satisfied:

> "If I stop, all I've got is just another seaplane. I don't have something that's a research breakthrough. And that's what I'm after. I'm seriously after something that we'll look back and say, 'what this airplane is and is able to do, in terms of operating in beaches, rough water, and have the kind of capabilities that it has, is not just something a little better than the best floatplane, but something that is really truly breakthrough in nature.'"

If all goes well with additional flight tests and reconfigurations, and Burt is satisfied with its performance, the final version of the SkiGull could be properly introduced to the flying world in 2017.

Figure 55   Burt Rutan's SkiGull.   Courtesy Burt Rutan

Figure 56   Burt Rutan and author in front of Burt's house in Idaho. From author's personal collection.

TIMELINE

1927 Charles Lindbergh begins his successful solo crossing of the Atlantic Ocean on December 14.

1938 Richard "Dick" Rutan born in Loma Linda, CA on July 1.

1943 Burt born June 17 in Estacada, OR.

1949 Family moves to Dinuba, CA, south of Fresno in California's Joaquin Valley.

1954 Dick Rutan receives his private pilot's license, the same day as his driver's license

1955 Burt builds first controline stunt model airplane.

Walt Disney's Disneyland first airs on television with episodes of *Man in Space* beginning on March 9.

1956 Burt builds a record-holding endurance controline model aircraft with nine-foot wing span.

Enters first WAM contest in San Francisco Bay area; it is the first of three successive years in this event.

1957 Opening of the motion picture, *The Spirit of St. Louis*, starring James Stewart.

1959 Burt solos in an Aeronca Champ and gets his private pilot's license.

Enters Nationals at Los Alamitos with a model of his father's Beech Bonanza.

1960 Enters Nationals at Dallas with 9 model aircraft including a Fokker-designed twin turboprop Fairchild F-27, Nordic Towline gliders A-1 and A-2 that may have been an inspiration for his now famous "Feathered Reentry" system conceived 43 years later.

Wins first place at the Nationals for the Fairchild F-27.

1961 Graduates from high school and enters California Polytechnic University at San Luis Obispo where he majors in aeronautical engineering.

Marries Judy Prather, his high school sweetheart.

1962 Designed first push-pull remote-controlled aircraft with Canard and tested a "VariViggen" design in a home-built wind tunnel.

Son, Jeffrey Albert Rutan, is born in August.

1963 X-15, flown by Joe Walker, breaks altitude record on August 22 by reaching 354,000 feet (107.8 km).

CalPoly seniors build a hybrid rocket motor for their senior project using Plexiglas as the solid fuel.

1964 Designs his first model with a canard configuration and assigns FX 935 as the tail number in honor of the SR-71 with a tail number of FX 934.

1965 Graduates from CalPoly and begins to work for the US Air Force at Edwards Air Force Base, becoming a Flight Test Project Engineer at the US Air Force Flight Center.

Daughter Dawn Rutan is born on August 30.

First EAFB project is the VSTOL XC-142A tilt-wing cargo aircraft.

Project on SC-142A with two controllers later in year.

1967   Begins testing VariViggen aerodynamics in homebuilt wind tunnel—the top of a fast-moving car!

Begins construction of the first VariViggen, the fabrication taking until 1971 to complete.

Is at Edwards AFB when Mike Adams, flying the X-15 reentered the atmosphere sideways, the craft disintegrated and he was killed.

First offensive against the American base at Khe Sanh, Viet Nam begins.

Begins flight test program on C-130 low level aero-delivery.

1968   Begins evaluation of Navy A-7 Corsair.

Begins flight test engineering work on stability and control of Phantom F-4E and develops revised procedures for spin and stall recoveries.

1970   Judy and Burt divorce and she takes his children, Jeff and Dawn.

1971   Spends five months at McDonnell Douglas flight test center in St. Louis, Missouri, working on F-4 and the new F-15 Eagle.

Marries Carolyn Weaver, a computer programmer at McDonnell Douglas, in St. Louis and returns with new family to Lancaster, California.

BD-5, a small one-seater microplane, makes its maiden flight in September.

Accepts an offer from Jim Bede to serve as director of testing and design of the Bede Flight Testing Center.

1972 Takes leave of absence from EAFB in March and moves to Valley Center, north of Wichita, KA to work for Jim Bede's Bede Aircraft Corp.

Fabrication of first VariViggen, Model 27, tail number N27VV is completed and first flight takes place on May 18.

Flies the VariViggen to the EAA air show at Oshkosh, Wisconsin in July.

Works on the Bede design of BD-5J and BD-5J Trainer.

1973 Bede BD-5J makes its first flight.

Establishes Rutan Air Factory (RAF) as a sole proprietorship for sale of VariViggen plans.

Flies the VariViggen to the EAA air show at Oshkosh, Wisconsin in July.

1974 Moves back to Mojave, CA in June and leases Building 13 for RAF.

Flies VariViggen for the movie *Death Race 2000* starring Sylvester Stallone and David Carradine.

Begins to draw initial plans for the VariEze.

1975 Motion picture *Death Race 2000* opens, featuring the VariViggen.

VariEze Proof of Concept craft, Model 31, tail number N7EZ makes its first flight on May 21.

Dick Rutan flies the VariEze to Oshkosh and lands on July 31 with Burt following in the VariViggen.

On August 4 Dick Rutan, flying the VariEze at Oshkos, breaks closed course world distance record for airplanes weighing under 500 kg by completing 1,638 miles.

1976 First flight of the VariEze, Model 33, tail number N7EZ, on March 14.

Installs an electric system on a VariEze.

Completes flight tests of the newly redesigned and reconfigured VariEze in June.

Begins selling the new VariEze, Model 33, in July.

1977 Designs and builds Quickie model 54, a single-seat homebuilt for Gene Sheehan and

Tom Jewett of Quickie Aircraft Corporation, with the first flight taking place November 17.

Designs NASA AD-1.

Pug Piper of Piper Aircraft Corporation asks Burt to develop a new plane, but Burt declines.

1978 Designs the Defiant, Model 40, tail number N78RA, a twin-engine, push-pull canard configuration, with the first flight taking place on June 30.

Builds solar water heating system for RAF.

Separates and subsequently divorces Carolyn.

1979 The Long-EZ, Model 61, tail number N79RA, a bigger but simpler plane to operate than the VariEze, makes its first flight on June 13.

Introduces the Defiant and the Long-EZ at Oshkosh in July.

Delivers the oblique-winged NASA AD-1 to the Dryden Flight Test Center in February and the first flight takes place on December 21.

Dick Rutan leaves the Air Force as a Viet Nam war hero with more than 300 combat missions goes to work for RAF.

1980 RAF is incorporated.

1981 Dick leaves RAF.

At dinner with Dick and Jeana Yeager, Burt suggests a plane to break the world distance record held by a B-52 set in 1962— Burt turns to his brother and asks, "How would you like to be the first person to fly around the world without stopping to refuel?"

1982 Establishes Scaled Composites LLC in April.

Contract signed on August 25 with Beech Aircraft Company to design the Starship.

Design and construction of Voyager begins in Hangar 77 at Mojave Airport.

Final flight of the AD-1 on August 7 at EEA in Oshkosh, WI.

In response to the 1982 Sailplane Homebuilders Association Design Contest for a homebuilt glider, Rutan designs and builds the first Model 77 Solitaire.

1984 Begins sales of the Defiant homebuilt.

Voyager makes its first test flight on June 22, 1984.

Voyager, piloted by Dick and Jeana, makes a long-distance, 11,600-mile four-day non-stop flight on a long pattern along California's Pacific Coast. Dick flies Voyager to the EAA airshow in Oshkosh at the end of July.

Dick and Jeana buy out Burt's half interest in the Voyager.

Marries Margaret Remblesake, daughter of a Beech Aircraft vice president.

1985 RAF stops selling plans for homebuilts, but continues to operate in support of builders.

Mike and Sally Melvill form a division of Scaled to do projects for Scaled using RAF facilities.

Burt and other investors sell Scaled to Beechcraft Aircraft Corporation in July.

1986 First production-sized model of the Starship flies on February 15.

Voyager lifts off from Edwards Air Force Base at 8:01 am on December 14 and return at 8:06 am on December 23 after completing the 24,986-mile non-stop flight.

President Ronald Regan awards Burt the Presidential Citizen's Medal on December 29.

1987 Award Grand Medal and National Medal of the Aero Club of France on January 29.

Receives the J.J. Doolittle Award from the Society of Experimental Test Pilots.

Receives the British Gold Medal for Aeronautics in December from the Royal Aeronautical Society.

On May 15, receives the Collier Trophy for ingenious design and development of the

Voyager and skillful execution of the first non-stop, non-refueled flight around the world.

Delivers commencement address at CalPoly in San Luis Obispo, CA, and finds that the wood bearings he installed in 1962 are still functioning.

Jim Walsh leaves Beechcraft and is succeeded by Max Bleck who seeks to end a number of Scaled projects including the Starship.

1988 Builds the Catbird, model 81, a high-efficiency five-seat single-engine all-composite aircraft for Beechcraft to replace the Beech Bonanza. First flight takes place on January 14.

Beech Aircraft sells Scaled to WUTTA, a company formed by Burt.

1989 Burt sells WUTTA to Wyman-Gordon Company in January.

In November *Popular Science* cover calls his desert Pyramid House the "21st Century House" and "the ultimate energy-efficient house."

1990 Ares Light Attack plane makes its first flight on February 19.

Builds the LIMA 1 with a Lexus engine on an Aztec test bed for Toyota; the first flight is in April.

1991 Designs the Pond Racer for Bob Pond; it makes its first flight on March 22.

The LIMA II, a new all-composite, high efficiency, low noise, 4-place light plane built for Toyota. It makes its first flight on November 4.

Earthwinds RTW Gondola makes its first flight in November.

1993 Catbird piloted by Dick Rutan wins the CAFE Challenge with a record score and a speed of 210.73 mph , fuel consumption of 20.15 mpg and a payload of 976.63 pounds.

On August 18, Delta Clipper-Experimental rocket, or DC-X, blasts off at 4:43 p.m. mountain time, flies to an altitude of 150 feet, stops, hovers, and moves laterally 350 feet.

Raptor D-1 Manned UAV POC first flight May 9.

Jet LongEZ makes its first flight in August.

Begins sketching his ideas for a rocket-powered capsule launched at high altitudes.

1994   Raptor D-2 makes its first flight on August 24.

Burt begins sketching plans for a craft that would exceed the speed of sound and leave the atmosphere—i.e. a spaceship.

Catbird sets two more world records in August and is subsequently retired.

1995   Begins the design of the Boomerang, an asymmetrical, piston propeller-driven twin-engine 300-knot airplane that would not become dangerously difficult to control in the event of failure of a single engine.

Begins working on the Proteus, a twin turbofan plane designed for enduring flights at very high altitudes (above 60,000 feet). The jet is designed for a multitude of missions, including reconnaissance, research, and hopefully for launching vehicles into space to carry passengers. It becomes the model for the White Knight in Burt's subsequent space ventures.

1996   The Boomerang makes its first flight on June 19.

Peter Diamandis announces Ansari $10 million X-Prize but the prize is not funded.

Approaches Vern Raburn at Oshkosh and asks him if Paul Allen might be interested in helping Angel Technologies develop broadband capability based on the Proteus.

Paul Allen flies down to Scaled Composites in September to meet Burt.

Burt registers for the X-Prize on May 18, at the Foundation's gala event.

Acquires a General Electric EV-1 for his primary car.

V-Jet II VLJ POC makes its first flight on April 13.

VisionAire Vantage makes its first flight on November 14.

1997 Mike Melville and Dick Rutan fly their LongEZs around the globe.

Singer John Denver is killed when he runs out of fuel in a LongEZ. The National Safety

Transportation Board absolves Burt of any responsibility or failure of Burt's design.

1998 Global Hilton RTW Gondola makes its first flight in January.

Unveils the Proteus on September 23.

First flight of the Proteus takes place on July 26.

Precision Cast Products Corporation acquires Wyman-Gordon Company for $721 million.

Burt meets with Paul Allen in Seattle to float the idea for a manned rocket flight into suborbital space.

More than 120 planes fly into Mojave, CA to celebrate Rutan's 55th birthday.

1999 Burt comes up with the idea of tilting the wings to a 65-degree angle to create the feathering necessary for carefree reentry.

Proteus Aircraft included in the list of the "100 Best of the Century," *Time Magazine*, April 1999.

Roton ATV Rotary Rocket makes its first flight in March.

2000   Burt and ten investors, including Dave Gruber and Mike Melvill, form Scaled Composites LLC in September and purchase the assets of the Scaled division of Precision Cast Products for $6 million.

Adam 209 Twin Reciprocal makes first its flight on March 21.

Proteus achieves highest altitude of 63,245 feet in October and breaks high altitude record.

Begins to think of using a winged craft instead of a space capsule to bring suborbital astronauts safely back to earth and begins exploring a feathering-form of reentry.

In the late Spring or early Summer, after coming up with the innovative concept of a feathering "carefree" reentry system, Rutan approaches Paul Allen about funding and they agree for Burt to develop the design and build two planes for a "minority equity stake."

Receives the Clarence L. "Kelly" Johnson "Skunk Works" award from the Engineers Council in February.

Receives the Lindbergh Award from the Lindbergh Foundation on May 20.

2001   Partnership between Paul Allen and Burt, called Mojave Aerospace Ventures LLC (MAV), is finalized in March. They call the secret project Tier 1 and the firm is dedicated to handling the commercial spinoffs from the Tier 1 efforts and to winning the X-Prize.

The roll-out ceremony of the X-47A, an unmanned combat vehicle, takes place in July.

2002 The Ansari X-Prize is finally funded through the purchase of a "hole-in-one" insurance policy by the Ansari family.

White Knight is prepped for its first flight in August.

Diagnosed with 10 percent or greater possibility of "sudden-death heart attack.

2003 Burt and nine other investors including Northrop Grumman acquire Scaled Composites from Wyman-Gordon, a subsidiary of Precision Cast parts Corporation.

Spaceship *Columbia* breaks up on reentry over Texas on February 1.

X-47A, built for DARPA, makes its first flight on February 23.

Rutan introduces SpaceShipOne to the public on April 18 with *White Knight* doing fly byes.

SpaceShipOne makes its first powered outing on the hundredth anniversary of the Wright brothers' first flight—December 17—the first time a non-prime aerospace company developed and flew a supersonic aircraft.

2004 Richard Branson approaches Paul Allen in March to seek a license to MAV's patented technology and to go after a full-fledged space program.

Capricorn GlobalFlyer makes its first flight in March.

At a dinner on June 20, Burt, Paul Allen and Sir Richard Branson discussed the possibility of working together on the development of private space travel.

On June 21 SpaceShipOne becomes the first privately built, flown, and funded manned craft to reach space.

Letter from the Smithsonian's National Air and Space Museum wanting to add SpaceShipOne to the Milestones of Flight gallery. Burt and Paul cancel all further flights.

In September, MAV signs a contract with Richard Branson's newly formed company Virgin Galactic, to establish The Space Ship Company for the purpose of developing a suborbital spacecraft for space tourism and to place the Virgin logo on all future craft pursuing the X-Prize.

SpaceShipOne makes the first flight for the Ansari X-Prize on September 29, reaching an altitude of 338,000 feet, well above the required minimum for space.

SpaceShipOne completes the second flight to space on October 4, five days after the first flight, reaching 367,500 feet, well above the 328,000 foot-minimum, and MAV wins the Ansari X-Prize

Burt and SpaceShipOne adorn the cover of *Time* magazine on November 29.

2005 National Aeronautic Association awards Burt et al the Collier Trophy for 2004 accomplishments associated with SpaceShipOne.

GlobalFlyer, an airplane built by Rutan and piloted by Steve Fossett, takes off on March 1 and circumnavigates of the globe on March 3 with a non-stop, non-refueled flight.

White Knight delivers SpaceShipOne to Oshkosh on July 25, followed by a trip to the Smithsonian.

In October SpaceShipOne is hung between The *Spirit of St. Louis* and the Bell X-1.

National Academy of Sciences awards Rutan the NAS Award in Aeronautical Engineering.

Northrup Grumman announces successful tests and demonstrations of the ability to release a 500-pound inert weapon, from the Proteus.

2006 Global Flyer begins another global circumnavigation on February 7 with Steve Fossett at the controls and completes the longest recorded non-stop manned flight in history—26,389 miles—landing on February 11.

Scaled Composites enters into joint venture agreement with Northrop Grumman to form Spaceship Company.

Virgin Galactic accumulates $13 million in deposits for rides on the VSS *Enterprise* at $200,000 a head.

2007 Northrup Grumman acquires the balance of 61 percent of SCI in a deal for about $100 million in cash.

During a cold flow test of a nitrous oxide injector on July 26, an explosion at Mojave Spacecenter kills three shop technicians and injures three others.

2008 Checks into emergency at UCLA Medical center and has heart surgery to remove the hardened pericardium enveloping his heart.

National Space Society awards Burt the Heinlein Award on May 30, the 12th such award given by the Society.

Richard Branson unveils *White Knight Two* on July 28 at the Mojave Spacecenter.

First flight tests of *White Knight Two* begin in September.

2009 Burt makes a presentation at the EEA Airventure in Oshkosh on July 29 on his thoughts on climate change, presenting a study called: "Non-Aerospace Research Quests of a Designer/ Flight Test Engineer."

2010 The *VSS Enterprise* completes its first glide flight in October.

2011 Proteus is flown in tandem with the Global Hawk to demonstrate feasibility of aerial fueling by unmanned aerial vehicles.

The BiPod makes its first flight hop on March 30.

Burt is selected for the 2011 Daniel Guggenheim Medal Award.

Burt retires on April 1.

SpaceShipTwo completes first full feathering reentry test in flight on May 4.

On May 23 the *Los Angeles Times* reports on the development of a new bomber for the U.S. based on Boeing's Phantom Ray, Northrop's X-47B or Lockheed's RQ-170 Sentinel.

Paul Allen announces the formation of Stratolaunch Systems with Burt Rutan and Mike Griffin on December 13.

FURTHER READING:

Books

Allen, Paul. *Idea Man* Portfolio, Penguin. 2011 .

Encyclopedia of World Biography Supplement. Vol. 20. Detroit, MI: Gale Group, 2000.

Linehan, Dan. *Burt Rutan and the Race to Space.* Zenith Press. 2011.

Linehan, Dan. *SpaceShipOne: An Illustrated History.* Zenith Press. 2009.

Periodicals

Bailey, John. "Rutan's Racer Has Wraps Removed." *Flight International* (April 10, 1991): p. 5.

Bigelow, Bruce V. "Rocket Plane Source of Pride for Designer, Poway, Calif., Firm." *Knight Ridder/Tribune Business News* (December 18, 2003): p. ITEM03352173.

Bigelow, Bruce V. "San Diego-Area Aircraft Designer Has a Qwest to Bring Space within Reach." *Knight Ridder/Tribune Business News* (April 29, 2003): p. ITEM03119032 .

Bostwick, Charles F. "Rutan Unveils Privately Funded Spacecraft." *Daily News* (Los Angeles) (April 19, 2003): p. N1.

Carreau, Mark. "Privately-Financed Team Will Try to Send Man into Space." *Knight Ridder/Tribune Business News* (June 3, 2004): p. ITEM04155061.

Cohen, David. "Burt Rutan: The Maverick of Mojave." *NewScientist* (January 28, 2010). http://www.newscientist.com/article/mg20527451.000-burt-rutan-the-maverick-of-mojave.html

Costello, Carol and Miles O'Brien. "The Rutan Brothers." *America's Intelligence Wire* (from CNN News) (December 17, 2003). This article can also be found online at http://www.cnn.com/TRANSCRIPTS/0312/17/lad.12.html

Cox, Jack. "Burt Rutan: an EAA Perspective." *Sport Aviation.* (April 2011).

"EAA Pays Tribute to Burt Rutan." http://www.airventure.org/news/2011/110724_burt_rutan.html

Hastings, Deborah. "Iconoclast of Aircraft Design Refuses to Work by the Book." *Daily News* (Los Angeles, CA) (July 8, 1996): p. SC1.

Lemonick, Michael D. "Voyager's Triumph; A Flying Fuel Tank Sets Records." *Time* (July 28, 1986): p. 53.

Meisler, Andy. "Slipping the Bonds of Earth and Sky." *New York Times* (August 3, 1995): p. C1.

Noland, David. "Burt Rutan and the Ultimate Solo." *Popular Mechanics* (February 2005).

O'Brien, Miles, Bruce Burkhardt, and Kathleen Koch. "Wright Stuff; A Century of Flight-Part 1." *America's Intelligence Wire* (from CNN News) (December 13, 2003). This article can also be found online at http://www.cnn.com/TRANSCRIPTS/0312/13/nac.00.html.

Park, Edwards. "The Voyager's Bid to Girdle the Globe Is No Mere Canard." *Smithsonian* (February 1985): p. 72.

Paur, Jason. "Burt Rutan Designs a Hybrid Flying Car." *Wired* (July 18, 2011).

"Pilot Guides Private Plane Out of Atmosphere, a First." *New York Times* (June 21, 2004).

Pollack, Andrew. "A Maverick's Agenda: Nonstop Global Flight and Tourists in Space." *New York Times*(December 9, 2003): p. G5.

"Private Rocket Plane Unveiled by Burt Rutan." *Advanced Materials & Composites News* (May 5, 2003).

Schmitz, Barbara A. "Full House Turns Out to See Burt Rutan." *Sport Aviation* (July 31, 2009).

Schwartz, John. "Private Space Travel? Dreamers Hope a Catalyst Will Rise from the Mojave Desert." *New York Times* (June 14, 2004).

Schwartz, John. "Burt Rutan and Richard Branson Unveil New Tourist Spacecraft." *New York Times* (January 23, 2008).

Schwartz, John. "Safety Lapse is Suggested in Fatal Blast at Test Site." *New York Times* (February 9, 2008).

Shapiro, Steve. "Burt Rutan: The Scaled Composites Years." *Sport Aviation* (May 2011).

Skeen, Jim. "Private Spaceship Makes Supersonic Flight from Mojave, Calif., Airport." Knight Ridder/Tribune Business News (December 18, 2003): p. ITEM03352038.

Stone, Brad. "Let's Go to Space! One Hundred Years After the Wright Brothers' Famous Flight, a New Breed of Entrepreneur Is Pushing New Technologies to Their Limits, Turning Science Fiction into Reality."*Newsweek* (October 6, 2003): p. 54.

Sugar, Jim. "Boomerang!" *Popular Mechanics* (November 1996): p. 50.

"Tier One: Rutan Enters the Space Race with a Radical Design Now in Testing." *Popular Science* (December 1, 2003): p. 42.

Willford, Neal. "Canard Design Considerations." *Sport Aviation* (November 2009): p. 57.

AWARDS RECEIVED BY BURT RUTAN

1. AIAA, First Place National Student Undergraduate Award. 1965.

2. USAF Air Medal (rare award for civilian), 1970.

3. Stan Dzik Design Contribution Trophy, Oshkosh 1972.

4. Omni Aviation Safety Trophy, 1973.

5. EAA Outstanding New Design, 1975, 1976 and 1978.

6. Dr. August Raspet Memorial Award, "Outstanding Contribution to the Advancement of Light Aircraft Design," 1976

7. *Flying/Business and Commercial Aviation*, 1978. Special Award "For a Lifetime Involvement in, Service to and Support of General Aviation."

8. Western Plastics Exposition, "Pacesetter Award," 1978.

9. Press Club of Antelope Valley, "Newsmaker of the Year," 1980.

10. *Aviation Week and Space Technology* magazine, Special Achievement - Laurels for 1981, for "Imaginative Ideas for Light, Energy-Efficient Aircraft Design."

11. *Business and Commercial Aviation* magazine, "Most Important Contribution to Aviation during 1984."

12. Beechcraft Legion of Honor Distinguished Service. July 11th, 1985.

13. ABC World News Tonight, "Person of the Week," July 18, 1986.

14. American Institute of Aeronautics and Astronautics, Aircraft Design Certificate of Merit for initiative and creativity in the development of the Starship and Voyager aircraft, October 1986.

15. Presidential Citizen's Medal presented by Ronald Reagan, December 29, 1986 for Mr. Rutan's design/development of the Voyager 'round-the-world aircraft. This was the 18th award of the Presidential Citizen's Medal since its inception in 1969.

16. FAI Gold Medal for Voyager Construction, 29 Jan 87.

17. "Grand Medaille" de' Aero-Club de France, (Grand Medal of the Aero Club of France), January 29, 1987.

18. Medal of the City of Paris, January 29, 1987.

19. The Aero Club of Washington, 1986 Aviation Achievement Award, 24 February 1987.

20. NASA Langley Research Center, Directors Award, 24 Feb 87.

21. Society of Plastics Engineers, Award for Unique and Useful Plastic Product, (Voyager), 7 May 1987.

22. Society of Plastics Industry, Special Achievement Award for the Advancement of Composites for the Voyager Flight, 9 May 1987.

23. Society of NASA Flight Surgeons, W. Randolph Lovelace Award, 13 May 87.

24. Academy of Model Aeronautics, Distinguished Service Award, 15 May 1987.

25. National Aeronautic Association and the National Aviation Club, 1987 Collier Trophy for ingenious design and development of the Voyager and skillful execution of the first non-stop, non-refueled flight around the world, 15 May 1987.

26. Aero Club of New England, Voyager Award, 25 Jun 87.

27. American Academy of Achievement, Golden Plate to America's Captains of Achievement, 27 Jun 87.

28. Experimental Aircraft Association and Milwaukee School of Engineering, Medal of Outstanding Achievement and Distinguished Leadership in Aerospace Engineering, 4 Aug 87.

29. Daedalians of Edwards Air Force Base, Citation of Honor, 15 Aug 87.

30. Society of Experimental Test Pilots, 1987 J. H. Doolittle Award for outstanding professional accomplishment in aerospace technology management of engineering, September 1987.

31. Aerospace Education Foundation Air Force Association Jimmy Doolittle Fellow. 1987.

32. Gathering of Eagles, Aviation Man of the Year, 17 Sep 87.

33. Charles Lindbergh Fund - San Diego Museum, Lindbergh Eagle Award, 24 Sep 87.

34. National Business Aircraft Association, Meritorious Service Award for 1987, 29 Sep 87.

35. United States Air Force Association, United States Air Force 40th Anniversary Award for Extraordinary Achievement, 1987.

36. Aero Club of New England Godfrey L. Cabot Award. 1987.

37. The City of Genoa, Italy, Christopher Columbus International Communications Medal, 12 Oct 87.

38. Distinguished Achievement Award, International Aerospace Hall of Fame, San Diego. 1987 & 2004.

39. American Society of Mechanical Engineers, Spirit of St. Louis Medal, 16 Dec 87.

40. Royal Aeronautical Society, British Gold Medal for Aeronautics awarded for outstanding practical achievement

leading to advancement in aeronautics for his original conception and successful design and development of the Voyager aircraft, December 1987.

41. Induction into the Wright Brothers First Flight Society Shrine. December 17, 1987.

42. The National Society of Professional Engineers, Outstanding Engineering Achievement in the NSPE 22nd Annual Outstanding Engineering Achievement Awards Competition, 27 Jan 1988.

43. *Design News* "Engineer of the Year for 1988," 8 March 1988.

44. Franklin Institute, Franklin Medal for 1987, 13 April 1988.

45. Intellectual Property Owners, Distinguished Inventor Award for 1987, 14 April 1988.

46. Hawthorne Chamber of Commerce, History of Aviation Award. August 27th, 1988.

47. Western Reserve Aviation Hall of Fame, Meritorious Service Award, 2 Sep 1988.

48. The International Aerospace Hall of Fame Honoree, 24 Sep 1988.

49. *Sailing World* Magazine, Medal of Achievement, January 1989.

50. Aero Club of Northern California, Crystal Eagle Award, 18 Mar 1989.

51. Secretary of the Air Force, Meritorious Civilian Service Medal for service on the USAF Scientific Advisory Board, April 1989.

52. Member of the National Academy of Engineering, 4 Oct 1989.

53. Leroy Randle Grumman Medal for outstanding scientific achievement 4 Oct 1989.

54. Professional Pilot Magazine, Star Performer. March 1990.

55. Structural Dynamics and Materials Award from American Institute of Aeronautics and Astronautics, presented "for innovative and outstanding contributions to the advancement of aerospace technologies, including the design, development and testing of light-weight, high performance composite structures materials," 14 April 1992.

56. Wings Over Houston Airshow Executive Committee, 1993 Lloyd P. Nolen Lifetime Achievement in Aviation Award, 16 Oct 1993.

57. Society for the Advancement of Materials and Process Engineering George Lubin Award, 9 May 1995.

58. National Aviation Hall of Fame Honoree, 21 July 1995.

59. SETP Ray E. Tenoff Award for Most Outstanding Paper. 1996

60. "Freedom of Flight" award for "contributions to EAA and to aviation, especially for his leadership in the design of recreational aircraft—including Voyager—that have had an impact on the international aviation community", Experimental Aircraft Association, 3 August 1996.

61. College of Engineering Medallion "in recognition of extraordinary leadership and commitment in support of the Aeronautical Engineering Department". April 18, 1997, The College of Engineering at Cal Poly, San Luis Obispo.

62. Chrysler Award for Innovation in Design. 1 October 1997

63. EAA Homebuilders Hall of Fame, 23 October 1998

64. MBA Ltd Sir James Martin Memorial Trophy. 1998

65. *Professional Pilot Magazine*, Aviation Designer of the Year Award. 13 March 1999

66. Proteus Aircraft included in the list of the "100 Best of the Century", *Time Magazine*, April 1999

67. Clarence L. "Kelly" Johnson "Skunk Works" award by the Engineers Council "to honor and perpetuate Kelly Johnson's qualities, accomplishments, standards and model of excellence to be aspired to by future generations of engineers, pioneering progress of the future." February 2000

68. 2000 Lindbergh Award presented by the Lindbergh Foundation for a shared vision of a balance between technological advancement and environmental preservation. May 20, 2000.

69. The 2001 J.H. "Jud" Hall Composites Manufacturing Award presented by the Composites Manufacturing Association of the Society of Manufacturing Engineers for his "contribution to the composites manufacturing profession through leadership, technical developments, patents and/or educational activities", 22 Feb 2001

70. The Reed Aeronautics Award presented by the American Institute of Aeronautics and Astronautics "in recognition of significant contributions and achievements in the field of aeronautical sciences and engineering, as an engineer, designer and builder of aircraft that challenge conventional wisdom, thus opening the door for innovation in aircraft prototyping and stimulation of new ideas and applications to further aerospace endeavors, May 9, 2001.

71. Laurel Legend Award presented by *Aviation Week & Space Technology*. Received award and was inducted into the *Aviation Week & Space Technology* Hall of Fame, April 16, 2002.

72. "100 Stars of Aerospace" (ranked 29th) presented by *Aviation Week & Space Technology*. Received award in Paris at Salle Wagram, June 18, 2003.

73. Popular Science Best Of What's New, for SpaceShipOne. 2003

74. "Business Leader in Aerospace" presented by *Scientific American* for designing a reusable sub-orbital passenger spacecraft. One of 50 individuals, teams or companies whose accomplishments in research, business or policy making during 2002-2003 demonstrate outstanding technological leadership, November 10, 2003.

75. Space Frontier Foundation Vision To Reality Award. 2004.

76. ACMD Composites Hall of Fame Honors. 2004.

77. Academy of Model Aerodynamics Model Aviation Hall of Fame.

78. Society of Experimental Test Pilots, "2004 J. H. Doolittle Award for outstanding professional accomplishment in aerospace technology management of engineering," September 2004. First to receive the Doolittle twice.

79. Society of Flight Test Engineers Kelly Johnson Award. September 2004

80. X Prize (Shared with key SS1 team and Paul Allen). For repeated private manned space flights. 4 October 2004.

81. State of Texas Honorary Texan. October 28th, 2004.

82. Charles A and Anne Morrow Lindbergh Foundation The Lindbergh Medal. November 6, 2004.

83. Damiano Colombo Meilano, Coniarioni d' Arte. 2004

84. *Wired Magazine's* "Rave Award" for Industrial Designer Burt Rutan. 22 Feb. 2005.

85. International Academy of Science Distinguished Fellow of Science. 2005.

86. Smithsonian's National Air and Space Museum's "Current Achievement Award". 9 March 2005

87. *Aviation Week and Space Technology* 2004 Laurel Legend Award for Innovation/Entrepreneurship. 19 March 2005

88. *Inc. Magazine* Entrepreneur of the Year

89. The Living Legends of Aviation Awards is the most important and prestigious recognition event in aviation. It's often referred to as the "Academy Awards of Aviation". Burt Rutan is a LLOA.

90. *Peabody award for Discovery's Two Black Sky documentaries 2004.*

91. The Explorers Club Medal. March 19th, 2005.

92. "Scientist of the Year" award by Achievement Rewards for College Scientists (ARCS). 15 April 2005.

93. *Time Magazine's "100 Most Influential People in the World".* 18 April 2005.

94. "2004 Robert J. Collier Trophy" - presented by National Aeronautic Administration, 19 April 2005. (This is the second Collier Trophy awarded to Rutan. Two others have multiple Colliers; Glenn Curtis and Kelly Johnson).

95. National Space Society Werner von Braun Memorial Trophy. May 2005.

96. California Polytechnic State University President's Medal of Excellence. September 2005.

97. Popular Mechanics 2006 Breakthrough Leadership Award. October 4th 2006.

98. Howard Hughes Memorial Award, 27th Recipient. 26 Jan 2006

99. Cooper-Hewitt 2005 National Design Award, Presented at White House by Laura Bush. 10 July 2006.

100. Asthma & Allergy Foundation Walk Of Fame Award. Breath Of Life Ball, 2006.

101. AIAA Space Transportation George Low Award. September 2006

102. 21st Century of Flight distinguished Award, San Diego Air & Space Museum Foundation. November 2006.

103. AIAA Engineer of the Year. 2007.
104. 2008 National Space Society's Robert A Heinlein Memorial Award.
105. Lifetime Achievement Award, Pasadena Art Center College of Design. 2009
106. 2009 Stanley Hiller, Jr Intrepid Pioneer Award. Oct 17, 2009.
107. Antelope Valley Press, Business Person of the Year. 2010
108. Antelope Valley Board of Trade Navigating Change Award. 2011.
109. Tribute to Burt Rutan at EAA's AirVenture, 2011
110. Flightglobal's Lifetime Achievement Award, 2011
111. Guggenheim Board of Award's 2011 Daniel Guggenheim Medal.

VIDEO AND OTHER MEDIA

There are a number of video and other graphic images at the Scaled Composites web site:
www.scaled.com

Burt Rutan and His Planes, Oshokosh AirVenture 2011
http://www.youtube.com/watch?v=6cxgb4tSkFQ&feature=youtu.be&hd=1

Burt Rutan Academy of Achievement 2004
http://www.achievement.org/autodoc/podcasts/artpod-7-rutan-vid?filterby=date_added

Burt Rutan.mov [At National Space Society]
http://www.youtube.com/watch?v=ENxro9wPkqc&feature=fvst

Big Think Interview With Burt Rutan
http://bigthink.com/ideas/18881

Turbon Killer Bee: Rutan ARES "Mudfighter" for U.S. Army Close Air Support
http://www.youtube.com/watch?v=zG9LlHcX8lg

Burt Rutan 1 of 8 SpaceShipOne
http://www.youtube.com/watch?v=TwDMAPwa8p8

Burt Rutan 2 of 8 Model Aircraft Competitions
http://www.youtube.com/watch?v=x3L7sACNeVs&feature=relmfu

Burt Rutan 3 of 8 Model Aircraft Competitions
http://www.youtube.com/watch?v=4fYnjCmqfYs&feature=relmfu

Burt Rutan 4 of 8 Designing at Edwards AFB
http://www.youtube.com/watch?v=SDHyg6pzkqI&feature=relmfu

Burt Rutan 5 of 8 First Home Built Airplane
http://www.youtube.com/watch?v=OzYPaWMI-do&feature=relmfu

Burt Rutan 6 of 8 BEDE Aircraft
http://www.youtube.com/watch?v=E787DxJB868&feature=relmfu

Burt Rutan 7 of 8 Rutan Aircraft Factory
http://www.youtube.com/watch?v=_TTz4yAF7Yc&feature=relmfu

Burt Rutan 8 of 8 Scaled Composites
http://www.youtube.com/watch?v=St3scZyyg3k&feature=relmfu

Rutan Birthday Bash 2008
http://www.youtube.com/watch?v=rozVcGROKk0&feature=related

Starship Times Two
http://www.youtube.com/watch?v=5T-QdXvARJ8&feature=related

Beech Starship 2000A Approach Landing at Santa Fe, NM
http://www.youtube.com/watch?v=SlMYg8C3cyk&feature=related

VariEze w/RV-7
http://www.youtube.com/watch?v=9xm7G66bVMg

VariEze N394WW Flight Test #5
http://www.youtube.com/watch?v=5_1K0l9lGjk

Long EZ
http://www.youtube.com/watch?v=4zOgEw-Lg5k

Rutan Firebird U/MCAV : U.S. Army CAS-MAS Candidate
http://www.youtube.com/watch?v=uTNEWCHCe10

Northrop Grumman X-47B First Flight UCAS-D (2011)
http://www.youtube.com/watch?v=dDnvxNdez84&feature=related

Ultimate Weapons X47B
http://www.youtube.com/watch?v=dyfjCgTUpq0&feature=related

Global Flyer
http://www.youtube.com/watch?v=Ml73lXW_jLs

Global Flyer
http://www.youtube.com/watch?v=Ml73lXW_jLs&feature=related

Tribute to Orbiter and SpaceShipOne
http://www.youtube.com/watch?v=m-mvWKDKDuo&feature=related

Virgin Galactic SpaceShipTwo
http://www.youtube.com/watch?v=APvW1OELo-k&feature=related

Virgin Galactic White Knight 2 Roll Out
http://www.youtube.com/watch?v=lepsTmxzuN4&feature=related

Virgin Galactic First Flight VSS Enterprise Captive First Flight
http://www.youtube.com/watch?v=rJJYjt5KF5g

Burt Rutan Sees the Future of Space
http://www.ted.com/talks/burt_rutan_sees_the_future_of_space.html

Burt Rutan: Entrepreneurs Are The Future of Space Flight
http://www.youtube.com/watch?v=nwfSENkvJXY

Big Think With Burt Rutan
http://bigthink.com/ideas/18881

Voyager:

This Day in History – Dec 23
http://tesla.liketelevision.com/liketelevision/tuner.php?channel=358&format=tv&theme=history

Voyager: Aviation's Last Great First
http://www.youtube.com/watch?v=ofw2dgGyHE8

Virgin Galactic's Space Program
http://mediagallery.usatoday.com/Virgin-Galactic's-space-program/G2190

Virgin Galactic –Milestones to Space.mov
http://www.youtube.com/watch?v=IRr0GLSAzdw&feature=yout
ube_gdata_player

Virgin Galactic Spaceship First Flight VSS Enterprise Captive
Carry Test Flight
http://www.youtube.com/watch?v=rJJYjt5KF5g&NR=1

Virgin Galactic Spaceship Two—Animation
http://www.youtube.com/
watch?v=APvW1OELo-k&feature=related

Spaceship Two
http://www.youtube.com/watch?v=XBlifr6EQNU&feature=related

Burt Rutan BiPod Update—Oshokosh 2011
http://www.youtube.com/watch?v=HSwkY5M4pPo&feature=
youtu.be&hd=1

Death Race 2000 trailer
http://www.mymovies.net/player/default.asp?filmid=604&url=/
trailers/movie.asp?qual=high,%20/filmmedia/film/fid604/trailers/
trid322/fh/high/high

Dinseyland's Men in Space TV series 1955;

Disneyland Man in Space Part 1 of 4
http://www.youtube.com/watch?v=ZWJrvT9sTPk

Disneyland Man in Space Part 2 of 4
http://www.youtube.com/watch?v=FNVXPOOY6pI&feature=rela
ted

Disneyland Man in Space Part 3 of 4
http://www.youtube.com/watch?v=PLLI9M3JvRc&feature=
related

Disneyland Man in Space Part 4 of 4
http://www.youtube.com/watch?v=gKv2Bz0xrKU&feature=related

Ekranoplan – Top Secret Technology From Russia
http://www.youtube.com/
watch?feature=player_embedded&v=dA0q1vCV0Ns#!
Ekranoplan – Caspian Sea Monster http://www.youtube.com/watch
?v=OeUe6aVib08&feature=related

Stratolaunch Systems, a Paul G. Allen Project
http://www.youtube.com/watch?v=sh29Pm1Rrc0

Other Media

Burt Rutan Climate Change Analysis
http://rps3.com/

History of the Long-EZ and the Rutan Aircraft Factory (Oshkosh
2010)
http://rps3.com/Files/Ochkosh_2010_talks/Long-EZ%20History.
pdf

Commercial Space – Our Future Opportunities
http://rps3.com/Files/Ochkosh_2010_talks/Commercial%20Space.
future%20opportunities.pdf

Innovation Creativity and Motivating Kids
http://rps3.com/Files/Ochkosh_2010_talks/Innovation.creativity.
Motivating%20Kids.pdf

Electric Flight Keynote
http://rps3.com/Files/Ochkosh_2010_talks/Electric%20flight%20
keynote.pdf

Egyptian Pyramids
http://www.burtrutan.com/burtrutan/downloads/Observations
PyramidFabricationTech.pdf.

Alien life and UFOs http://www.burtrutan.com/burtrutan/down-
loads/RutanIntroToJohnAxexanderUFOBook.pdf

PRAISE FOR DANIEL ALEF'S TITANS OF FORTUNE COREVIEW BIOGRAPHICAL PROFILES

"The great American automobile pioneers played a major role in creating the nation we have today and Daniel Alef s book, *A Road Well Traveled,* brings to life their stories, achievements, successes and, at times, failures. Some were mechanical geniuses; others great businessmen who could sell their dreams and make them come true. Anyone passionate about cars, vintage, antique or classic, and there are millions of us, will find a mother lode of information in this well written book."

— Andy Granatelli, "Mister 500" and automotive icon

"As the reader will learn, the automotive pioneers outlined in the following stories may represent the first group of true industrial entrepreneurs and may actually set examples of what can be accomplished today to rebuild our industrial base."

— Thomas T. Stallkamp, Former Vice Chairman and President of DaimlerChrysler Corporation.

"I've read these wonderful profiles with such pleasure...

— Barnaby Conrad, International best-selling author and founder of the Santa Barbara Writers Conference

"Your column on Otis Chandler was the best encapsulation of Otis I have ever seen."

— Marylin Chandler De Young, wife of Otis Chandler.

"I am a great fan of Titans of Fortune ... Dan Alef has found a savvy combination of facts and feelings in selected bios

— Fred Klein, Former executive editor at Bantam Books.

"As a fellow lawyer and writer, I was impressed with your easy style and eye for detail, and fluid prose—two hallmarks of a good storyteller.

— Pierce O'Donnell, Author of *Fatal Subtraction* and In *Time of War.*

"A friend of mine, who lives in Santa Barbara, sent me the copy of Capt. Matson, that was printed in your paper. It was beautifully written and I will put it in my keepsakes. I am a granddaughter of the Capt.; my father was Walter Matson ...

— Carol Park

"For a long time, I have enjoyed your essays. They are concise, well-written and informative. I think we do not tell writers often enough how much we appreciate their work, so I thought I would drop you a line.

— Mashey Bernstein, Lecturer, Writing Program at University of California at Santa Barbara

"It was fun to see you, especially as your mind was still churning Getty's life story, and then ... bam, it was there. You have a great reportial touch.

— Doran William Cannon, Award-winning Hollywood screenwriter, author and founder of The Writers Academy

Author Bio

Daniel Alef has written many legal articles, one law book, one historical anthology, *Centennial Stories*, and authored the award-winning historical novel, *Pale Truth* (MaxIt Publishing, 2000). *Foreword* Magazine named *Pale Truth* book of the year for general fiction in 2001 and the novel received many outstanding reviews including ones from *Publishers Weekly* and the American Library Association's *Booklist*. He is also a contributor to Sage Publishing's reference work *Gender and Women's Leadership*.

Titans of Fortune, biographical profiles of America's great moguls, men and women who had a profound impact on America and the World, began in April 2003. Mr. Alef's experience as a lawyer, CEO of a public company, a rancher, and author, combined with his academic background—UCLA (B.S.), UCLA Law School (J.D.), the London School of Economics and Political Science (LL.M.), and Cambridge University (post-graduate studies)—gave him the perception to analyze the powerful titans and their achievements, and to place their lives and triumphs in a larger perspective. The *Titans of Fortune* series of articles appeared in several newspapers including the Lee Newspapers, Knight-Ridder, and became a weekly column in the *Santa Barbara News Press*.

Today, digital editions of many of these biographical profiles are available on the major ebook platforms including the Kindle, iPad, Nook and Kobo, and constitute best-selling titles on Amazon and the iBookstore.

Mr. Alef has appeared on Bio.com, Discovery, MSNBC, and the History Channel. He has also been a guest speaker and lecturer at various university, Rotary, and Kiwanis clubs, public libraries including San Francisco and Chicago, cruise ships, and at numerous historical societies across the nation. Mr. Alef served on the Board of Trustees of the Santa Barbara Historical Museum, the UCSB History Associates Board of Directors and on the Board of Trustees of the Santa Barbara Sheriff's Activities League. He is a black belt in judo. He currently lives with his family in New Jersey and California.

BOOKS AND BIOGRAPHICAL PROFILES BY DANIEL ALEF

Pale Truth, award-winning historical novel of America and California

Sold! How America's Greatest Marketing and Sales Titans Pulled it Off

The Great Creators: Profiles of America's Remarkable Inventors and Innovators

Igor I. Sikorsky: Big Dreams, Big Planes, and the Rise of Helicopters

Jack Northrop: King of Wing

Clarence L. "Kelly" Johnson: From Skunk Works to the Edge of Space

Howard Hughes: The Mysterious Billionaire

William Edward Boeing: Sky King

Captain Eddie Rickenbacker: Ace of Aces

Juan Terry Trippe: Founder of Pan Am and Commercial Aviation

Anthony Fokker: The Flying Dutchman

Jackueline Cochran: Sky Queen

The Loughead Brothers: Aeromotive Innovators

Elon Musk: SpaceX, Tesla, and the Holy Grail

Mark Zuckerberg: The Face Behind Facebook and Social Networking

Steve Jobs: The Apple of Our i

Walt Disney: The Man Behind the Mouse

Jeff Bezos: Amazon and the eBook Revolution

Henry Ford: An American Icon

William Randolph Hearst: Media, Myth and Mystique

John D. Rockefeller, Sr.: America's First Billionaire

Sam Walton: Changed the World of Merchandising

Cornelius Vanderbilt: The Colossus of Roads

Andrew Carnegie: Prince of Steel and Libraries

George Eastman: The Kodak King

J. Edgar Hoover: Head of the FBI and the Seat of Government

Armand Hammer: An Oil Baron of Many Contradictions

More Daniel Alef biographical profiles are available on Amazon (Kindle), Apple iBookstore, Barnes and Noble, Kobo, and other ebook retailers.

Made in the USA
Monee, IL
02 January 2020